CLASSIC GUITAR

By Christopher Berg

MEL BAY PRESENTS

MASTERING GUITAR TECHNIQUE: PROCESS & ESSENCE

D1289675

EDITIONES CLASSICAE

Visit us on the Web at http://www.melbay.com — E-mail us at email@melbay.com

Contents

2

About the Author

Christopher Berg is a guitarist of uncommon ability. Audiences throughout the United States have been charmed by his technical mastery and compelling interpretations. Critics have praised his "superb mix of strong, deft technique and emotional intensity…" (The State) and "special sensitivity" (The New York Times). The News and Courier of Charleston, SC labeled him an "awesome talent," following his appearance during Spoleto '93.

He received his training at the Peabody Conservatory of Music with Aaron Shearer and in masterclasses with Andrés Segovia at the University of Southern California. He has been honored by the National Endowment for the Arts, as a recipient of a Solo Recitalist Fellowship, and by the South Carolina Arts Commission, as a recipient of two Solo Artist Fellowships. He is currently a professor of music at the University of South Carolina where he directs classical guitar studies. His students have won top prizes in regional and national performance competitions.

Acknowledgments

I don't think I have ever encountered a fellow guitarist, either teacher or performer, from whom I've been unable to learn. Sometimes the lessons have been positive, showing me qualities worthy of emulation and development. Occasionally, though, I would see certain attitudes and beliefs that held their owners back. These experiences helped me see the same traits within myself and invited me to change.

I have also learned from my students over the years. They may be surprised to learn of their role as my teachers, but it seems as if each of them, no matter what level, had a specific lesson for me.

There are many other friends, past and present, who have somehow assisted or witnessed my growth as a person. Many will never know their influence upon me and their importance in my life, but I must make a special acknowledgment to Georgia Cowart, who read this manuscript and offered valuable support and advice. Her unpublished manuscript, *Nurturing Knowledge,* written with Alisa Belflower, served as a catalyst to transform many of my ideas about teaching and learning. The work and example of these two people continue to have a profound effect on my life.

Finally, I am grateful to Aaron Shearer, my teacher from 1971-1977. If the teachings he offered me then were seeds, then the soil of my experience has nourished their growth in many ways expected and unexpected. Both owe a debt to his work.

All of you have been my teachers and I thank you.

3

Prelude

Process and Essence

True artists/learners have developed the curiosity and openness to continue learning the same things over and over again, but at higher and higher levels. For them, learning proceeds vertically along an ascending spiral path rather than linearly along a horizontal path. On the horizontal path, seating and the positioning of the guitar may be followed by the positioning of the hands, which is in turn followed by simple finger movements to produce sounds on the guitar. As other skills are learned there may be no understanding of the need to study seating and the positioning of the guitar again (or any previously studied area of guitar technique) at a higher level. This process of restudying material is not going back. It is going forward because our previous learning has changed us.

How does learning change us?

It puts us in a new place. We are able to see from a perspective we could not hold before. This new perspective allows us to process and absorb experience in a new way, whether that experience comes to us through imitation, information, sensation, intuition, or inspiration.

Imitation is the attempt to copy what we perceive to be the manifestation of another's experience. It often is the way most beginners are comfortable learning. It can be a highly efficient way of absorbing and processing material. But because beginners can only focus on the physical expression of another's experience, their learning may be superficial.

Imitation is not limited to beginners. Advanced students are often able to learn by imitating certain qualities, such as ease or grace. This can be a wonderful way of nonverbal learning.

Even when a gifted teacher can express the essence of her knowledge, creativity, or wisdom, to her students, it can only be experienced by them as information. Until students work with this information, it will remain dull and inert. Students are responsible for processing this information, for moving it through conscious practice, along their own path.

It may take many years before our physical sensations emerge as reliable guides to a new direction. Sensations often become contaminated by ineffective habits, rigid adherence to inappropriate information, or excessive muscular tension. We practice to acquire skills, but we also practice to restore or preserve the integrity of our sensations.

Intuition helps us when we suddenly can trust our sensations and ideas. We block our intuition when we believe that practicing, or any learning, is mechanical.

Sometimes we experience a sudden awakening of our possibilities. These joyful experiences usually occur after witnessing a particularly exciting performance, or after contact with a dynamic teacher. All of a sudden we can play better. Our technique flows more easily. We are able to make creative and dramatic musical gestures. These inspirational experiences are unearned and are difficult to retain. They may fade after several hours or days. They are afforded to us so we may glimpse and experience our possibilities. It is then up to us to grow into the truths we have seen.

Imitation, information, sensation, intuition, and inspiration can be understood as different levels of the learning spiral.

What does this mean?

This means that different things are true, but at different levels. For example, beginning students usually need to be offered teaching that will help them learn to hold onto notes formed by the fingers of the left hand. This is so they can learn to develop smooth connections between notes. As they progress and reach a certain level of speed, it is time for them to learn to let go. There are times when they must consciously think "let go" if they are to enter the realm of effortless virtuoso technique.

Sometimes the teaching offered a student is inappropriate for that student's level. When this happens the student will not be able to learn and may become confused. A teacher may explain an area of guitar technique by saying, "Do what feels right." What she is saying may help her

4

student. But if the student is unable to experience that area of guitar technique through his sensations, he will not be able to learn. The teacher is not wrong, but she has not recognized that her learning is at a different place on the spiral than that of her student. Another teacher may give his student more specific information about an area of technique. If the student can process that information intellectually, then apply it to herself and transform it through her experiences into knowledge, we can say she has learned. If she then, on her own, transfers that learning to solve new problems, we can say that she is creative.

Sometimes the teaching offered to beginners needs to be transformed as students become more advanced. When a beginner is first learning to use the left hand to play the notes e, f, and g on the first string, he is usually advised to keep the inside of his palm parallel to the side of the fingerboard. This is good advice—for the time being. As the student progresses, good teachers will follow up this teaching so the student learns flexibility and the reasons for it, in the way the arm presents the hand to the fingerboard.

Beginning students rarely possess trustworthy sensations. Often they will only be able to learn the outer shell or superficial form of a position or movement. This is fine in the beginning. Students may not be sensitive to the feel of minimal effort in their right-hand finger strokes. They may work too hard while stroking the string and they may have to use conscious effort to extend the finger for its next stroke. There will be a time when it will be appropriate to introduce the concept of ballistic movement. In this type of movement the student learns how to instantly replace the muscular contraction with a relaxation. This allows the finger to sail through its movement as a result of the initial contraction. Only then will the finger be free to simply release back to its midrange position with little discernible effort.

There is no need for these apparently "irreconcilable" teachings to cause confusion or divisiveness among guitarists. These different teachings are compatible when seen as part of the same process. Which one is "true" for us depends on where we are in our learning.

It is important for us to learn to suspend judgment about teachings from which we are unable to learn. When we judge them, we become closed to them. There may be a day when those teachings are exactly what we need.

It is always important to try to know where we are in our learning. Our successes as students and teachers depend on our ability to know where we are. A student's perception of where he is may not be accurate. It may be contaminated by unhealthy motivations or unrealistic expectations or denial. Good teachers compassionately reflect back to students the truth of where they are. Good teachers meet their students where they are and then take them forward into the unknown.

Good students are willing to go.

How do we make this journey into the unknown? What path do we take?

Imagine that one day you discover a big, beautiful and important book. On the cover of this book is your name, followed by the words, "Your Path To Complete Artistry." Imagine the value of such a book, an individual and compassionate curriculum for the joyous mastery of technique and musicianship, written just for you, tailored to your exact needs.

There is such a book. There is one for each of us.

We are unable to recognize this book because it does not exist in physical form. The pages of this book are written on our mistakes, our problems, our fears, and the places where we have become stuck. Every time we sit down to practice, we are given the choice to open this book or to ignore it. We alone decide.

Sometimes we have difficulty reading this book. It seems as though it is written in Latin and we only speak French. Some words will look similar to words we already know, but we may not understand their context. We need to learn to read this new language.

How does this happen?

We make a conscious choice to learn. We accept that improvement and growth require change.

Change occurs through the responsible choices that we make. These choices arise out of our willingness to experience our work from the different levels of imitation, information, sensation, intuition, and inspiration, rather than to experience our work as a repetition of the same things we have been doing. Practice is only useful insofar as it provides us the opportunities to make choices.

This means that if you have a problem playing scales, and you decide that all you need to do is to practice scales more, you have chosen to believe that technique, or any learning, is mechanical. This is simplistic thinking. Learning is organic. We must never forget that it is alive. It is alive because it responds so beautifully to the choices we make. This means that as you practice scales you become sensitive to the choices you can make to bring about change. Every facet of scale playing is subject to change based on your openness to imitation, information, sensation, intuition, and inspiration. This is how we improve and grow.

We must also openly invite the possibility that we can make a wrong choice, a mistake in direction. Stripped of judgmental connotations, "wrong" simply means that we have made a choice that takes us farther from our potential rather than closer to it. Our willingness to see and accept our "wrong" choices will teach us the important things that we need to learn before we can continue.

It is this process, the process of responsible choice, that will lead us to essence.

There can be no justification for all the attention given process in this book, unless it can lead us to essence. The essence of any art is truth. Performance occurs in a sacred space, and all sacred spaces demand that we rise to a level of truth unobtainable in our daily lives. Our preparation before we enter this space will determine the level of truth and authenticity we are able to reach.

Part of this truth is that which connects us, binds us together: our humanity, fragility, and the integrity of our responses. Any attempt to manipulate the audience or produce an effect or an image will eventually require more and more energy to sustain itself.

True artists have cultivated their physical, emotional, intellectual, and spiritual sensitivity to music. They are able to find their deep and meaningful responses to music, and their technique has developed in such a way so they can express these authentic responses to their audiences.

It is my heartfelt hope that this book will help you discover the freedom to make the choices that will bring you closer to the guitarist and musician you can be, no matter where you are in your own learning.

Preface

This is not a method or self-instruction book for beginners. It was created to serve as a supplement to many of the method and technique books already available. It assumes a modest music reading ability and some familiarity with the more superficial aspects of classical-guitar technique. It contains no repertoire; its aim is to introduce concepts, as well as exercises and procedures for the practical application of those concepts, to aid the development of a musically-sensitive technique. It is intended for guitarists who, perhaps after years of playing, have become inquisitive and serious about their technique and their ability to play music.

This does not exclude others from using it. Teachers of beginners can use this book as a text offering added, and in some cases alternative, technical information. More advanced students can use this book to evaluate their technique and to develop the tools and resources needed to solve many of the unique problems facing the serious guitarist. It should, in most cases, be used with a qualified teacher; there is no substitute for the elaboration and clarification teachers can provide.

If properly studied, this material will help dedicated students develop a refined and musically-responsive technique. This technique will not only allow control of the guitar, but will, through the elimination of uncomfortable and unneeded tension, be sensitive enough to respond to the most subtle interpretive idea. The implications and ultimate purpose of this volume can only be fully realized through the study of music.

The development of an advanced and musically-sensitive technique must begin with the consideration of the most elementary aspects of positioning and movement. In many respects there is no such thing as advanced technique, only degrees of mastery of simple movements. Although students often try to develop the quantity of their technique through exercises and etudes, the quality of technique can be improved only by understanding, applying, and mastering concepts of positioning and movement.

This requires that we put our hands in a series of increasingly challenging "technical environments." Our sensitivity, intuition, and intellect should help us make any adjustments in positioning and movement to comfortably succeed in those environments. Repetition and drill can then help establish beneficial reflexes and habits.

It is difficult to isolate and discuss each particular facet of guitar technique. Each area and improvement will logically grow out of the development and cultivation of earlier skills. What we are capable of at any given time is the result of past study and will affect our future growth. Ideally, through the application of accurate technical information, the evolution and development of a superior technique should seem inevitable. But technique rarely develops in so efficient a manner. Students and teachers sometimes become sidetracked, or are simply not skilled in diagnosing and solving problems—a skill that is dependent on the recognition of the relationships between the various areas of technique to each other, and their relationship to our ability to perform music. A consideration of the mechanical possibilities and limits of ourselves is the place to begin.

Our Primary Instrument

Introduction

Teachers and their students need to be aware of the dangers of trying to explain individual elements of guitar technique as abstractions separate from music. There are many pitfalls in trying to describe physical sensations to others; it is not unlike trying to send a kiss by messenger. But the ability to separate the means from the end is essential if technique is to progress beyond the most rudimentary level—the quality of the means will determine the quality of the end.

There are many guitar books available, and they all try to deal with the use of the guitar. Few are committed to a sustained effort to uncover information about ourselves and to apply that information to the requirements of a musically-sensitive technique. Some of these books try to describe the full-blown technique used by different masters, without exploring how or why the technique developed as it did. Others are pedagogical potpourris of directives masquerading as principles.

Serious guitar students need concrete and reliable information that can help them solve their technical and musical problems. When students come seeking advice and training, teachers and performers must give them information and ways of applying that information, that will not sabotage their future with the instrument. In many cases, damage from misuse (often misdiagnosed as overuse) will not show up until years later, usually after contact with a teacher has ceased. A 1985 study of serious musculoskeletal problems in high-level musicians revealed that the "mean age of those reporting injuries was 30 years and the median years of playing experience at symptom onset was 12 years."[1]

The current interest in arts medicine has made many aware of the serious problems that can occur through the misuse of (in the words of Dr. Richard Norris, Medical Director of the *National Arts Medicine Center* at the National Rehabilitation Center in Washington, DC) "the instrument we use to play our instrument." All too often what is seen as a lack of talent or industry is a lack of sound training. Guitarists seem to have an especially hard time of it. Dr. Rauol Tubiana of the *Institut Français de la Main* in Paris writes: "Because of both position and technique, the guitarist has a greater variety of inherently anti-physiological gestures than do most other instrumentalists."[2]

My purpose in the first part of this book is to present information about the abilities and limits of the different parts of our body; to explore the relationship between the function of our central nervous system and how we practice; and finally, to distill these discussions into several technical principles. Dr. Frank R. Wilson, a neurologist with an interest in the training and development of musicians, puts it this way: "If you were never going to undertake anything more complex than combing your hair, it would not make any difference whether you understood how you are able to manage your own grooming. However, it makes a great deal of sense to know something about what's under your hood if you intend to explore the limits of your own physical capabilities, or want to understand why some efforts succeed and others do not."[3]

These observations on efficient physiologic and neurologic function can aid the development of an effortless and musically-sensitive guitar technique. My hope is that many guitarists will find this information as interesting and as useful as I have. This material has given me confirmation and a deeper understanding of certain areas of my training and "technical instincts"; it has also given me the insight and the means to question and change other areas.

The twenty-four lessons[4] which follow explore the application of many of the concepts presented here to specific areas of guitar technique.

---

1) Paul H. Caldron, D.O., et. al., *Medical Problems of Performing Artists,* Vol. 1, No. 4, December 1986, 139.
2) Raoul Tubiana, M.D. and Phillippe Chamagne, L. P.T., and Roberta Brockman, M.D., "Fundamental Positions for Instrumental Musicians," *Medical Problems of Performing Artists,* Vol. 4, No. 2, June 1989, 76.
3) Frank R. Wilson, *Tone Deaf and All Thumbs,* (New York: Vintage Books, 1987), 25.
4) The organization of material into lessons is not intended to represent a schedule of ideal weekly progress. The pace and sequence of the material is best left to the teacher. The division of each area of study into lessons is simply for convenience.

The Use of the Self[5]

Frank Pierce Jones, a research psychologist and pupil of F. Matthais Alexander, wrote in the January 1, 1949 issue of *Musical America:*

> There are musicians—some say there were more of them in the past—who get as much pleasure from a performance as they give, who always perform easily and well, and who use themselves so efficiently that their professional lives and their natural lives coincide. There are others, however, with equal talent and training, to whom performance and even practice are exhausting, and whose professional lives are cut short because they lose the mastery of the skills they have acquired. They put forth more effort in solving technical problems than the results warrant, and ultimately discover that they have used up their reserves of energy. If they understood the use of themselves as well as they understand the use of their instruments, such breakdowns would be far less frequent.[6]

The "use of the self" includes understanding the influence our positions have on our ability not only to move, but to develop increasing levels of sensitivity to movement. The more sensitive we are to movement, the more sensitive we can become to music. The use of the hands and fingers, or any other part of the body, including the central nervous system, is closely linked to the way the body as a whole is used.

Some positions and movements are favorable and efficient because they are mechanically advantageous and physiologically normal. Others are unfavorable and at best, inhibit the development of technical fluency, and at worst, put the guitarist at risk for the development of serious and often debilitating problems. The function of the legs, lower back, torso, neck, and head, and the joints of the arm, wrist, and fingers, and their muscles, should be of the utmost concern to serious guitarists. If guitarists properly understood the relationships between these parts and the importance the central nervous system and brain have in their development, the study of guitar technique would be a joyous process of discovery rather than the frustrating battle it often is.

Positioning the Body • • • • •

The first problems facing the guitar student are seating and the positioning of the guitar. Traditional methods recommend the student put the left foot on a footstool, position the guitar on the left thigh, and *then* manipulate the torso to bring the hands to the instrument. This often includes collapsing the lower back, leaning and turning the torso to the left, dropping the shoulders, and twisting the neck. A mechanically advantageous position will seek to preserve the alignment of muscles with their joints, of nerves with the areas they supply, and of the spinal column with the brain. This means keeping both feet on the floor so the legs can release away from the pelvis, the back straight so the spine is allowed to lengthen and the torso widen, and the head resting lightly on the neck. Once this alignment has been attained, the guitar can then be positioned respecting the body (with the help of some sort of guitar support) so this advantageous position can be maintained—even when playing in the upper positions.

The relationship between the neck and head was the cornerstone of Alexander's work. Frank Pierce Jones continued his article with a brief description of Alexander's work:

> To my knowledge, Alexander was the first expert, working with human beings in ordinary activities of life, to show and prove that there is what he called the "primary control" within each individual. He defines the primary control as "a certain use of the head and neck in relation to the rest of the body." By observation and experiment upon himself, "using," as John Dewey said, "the strictest scientific method," he learned that the mechanism that determines the character of all reflex action lies in the reflexes governing the relation of the head to the neck. When the primary control is functioning as it should, it is sensed as an integrating force that preserves freedom of movement throughout the system, so that energy can be directed to the place where it is wanted without developing strain either there or elsewhere. Misuse of this control, on the other hand, is always reflected by misuse somewhere else: this appears in the form of awkwardness, fatigue, and what Wilfred Barlow, a London physician and pupil of

---

5) This title of this section is borrowed from: F.M. Alexander, *The Use of the Self,* (New York: Dutton, 1932).
6) This article appears as an appendix in Frank Pierce Jones', *Body Awareness in Action,* (New York: Shocken Books, 1976), 182.

Alexander, calls, "maldistributed muscle tension," or over-tension at one place accompanied by under-tension at another.[7]

The discovery of a seating position that allows proper "use of the self" while playing should be explored in detail by serious guitarists before they try to develop patterns of movement for their arms and hands (see Lesson One).

The Arms and Hands • • • • • • • •

The function of each joint and its muscles remains constant from one physiologically normal individual to another.[8] Knowledge of these functions can contribute to the development of important technical principles. Although the arms, and especially the hands and fingers, are in continuous use during guitar playing, their positions and movements are often given little intelligent thought. Guitarists often proceed on the assumption their hands will "naturally" adopt the best way for them,[9] or they become adept at imitating *what they perceive* to be the positions and movements of accomplished performers, without understanding what went into developing these positions and movements or taking account of important physical differences.

The Arm

The hand lies at the end of a chain of three major joints, the shoulder, elbow, and wrist, and two nearly equal segments, the upper arm and forearm. The positions and movements of the arm and wrist are responsible for the presentation of the fingers and hands to the guitar.

The **shoulder** is the most mobile joint of the body.[10] Proper positioning (a function of seating) and movement from this joint are important to shifting along the fingerboard for the left hand and string crossing for the right hand. The arm movements for these techniques should come from the shoulder, but the shoulder itself should not move. Movement from the shoulder can also move the left elbow toward or away from the body—this repositioning of the left hand can simplify problems of reach and accuracy.

The **elbow** connects the upper arm to the forearm and moves in only one plane. Movement from the

elbow (in conjunction with movement from the shoulder) allows the arm to continuously adjust its length.[11] In left-hand technique this joint is usually kept in its midrange position between the limits of flexion and extension. In right-hand technique the flexion and extension of the forearm will naturally accompany arm movement from the shoulder during string crosses. Movements from the elbow and wrist alone are sometimes used for string crossing during brief scale passages or during scale work on the bass strings.

The construction of the **forearm** allows a comfortable rotation over its entire length. The movements for this rotation, which arise at the wrist, are *pronation* and *supination.* Many guitarists make use of these movements by cultivating a slight inward[12] tilt of the right forearm (pronation). An excessive inward tilt, however, may introduce the debilitating effects of the "quadrige phenomenon" to the middle finger, especially during arpeggios. (See page 16.) An inward tilt may permit the thumb to work more effectively and may be a part of beginning technique, but guitarists will eventually need to develop the sensitivity to experiment. Aaron Shearer suggests that an inward tilt reduces problems caused by the different lengths of the i and m fingers.[13] But the i finger has a greater range of extension than either the m or a finger (see page 16) and can function very effectively without a tilt. Because the fingers (especially i and m) do not have the same range of movement, their midrange positions will vary. Many great players play rest stroke with their i finger extended slightly while their m finger is more curved. It is a mistake to force the fingers to have the same angles at their joints. Other guitarists have suggested that the tilt is related to the relative lengths of i and a: if i is shorter than a (which is the case for most people), a slight inward tilt (pronation) may be required; if a is shorter than $i,$ a slight outward tilt (supination) may be required; if i and a are equal in length, no tilt may be needed.[14] What may be more important, however, is to position the wrist at its midrange between the extremes of pronation and supination. Even a slight inward tilt approaches the limit of pronation.

Left-hand technique will often require a slight rotation of the left forearm to help position the fourth

7) Jones, 184.
8) A discussion of anatomical variations will be presented later.
9) See the discussion of "The Natural Approach" in Aaron Shearer's *Learning the Classic Guitar, Part One,* (Pacific, Mo.: Mel Bay Publications, Inc. 1990), 117. Also see Hector Quine, *Guitar Technique,* (New York, NY, Oxford University Press, 1990), 4.
10) Raoul Tubiana, *The Hand, Vol. 1* (Philadelphia: WB Saunders, 1982), 19.
11) Raoul Tubiana, M.D. and Phillippe Chamagne, P.T., "Functional Anatomy of the Hand," *Medical Problems of Performing Artists,* Vol. 3, No. 3, September 1988, 83.
12) Directional terms for right-hand positioning follow those established by Aaron Shearer in *Learning the Classic Guitar,* 30.
13) Shearer, 33.
14) Pepe Romero, *Guitar Style and Technique,* (New York: Bradley Publications, 1982), 8.

finger toward the bass strings (supination) or the first finger toward the bass strings (pronation) *without the fingers having to reach.* These movements, either by themselves for simple textures, or combined with a movement of the left elbow toward or away from the body for more difficult chord shapes, can allow the left-hand fingers to maintain an efficient position. This "dynamic positioning" allows a flexible and ever changing presentation of the angle of the hand to the fingerboard (hence the term "dynamic") while preserving a mechanically advantageous position of the wrist and fingers. This position of mechanical advantage is defined by the alignment and midrange principles, at least as a point of departure. (These will be fully explored later.) The ability to take advantage of this flexibility is dependent on the angle and height of the neck of the guitar.

The dynamic positioning of the left hand is neither new nor unusual; many fine guitarists and teachers have recognized that the diverse positions and type of movements required of the left hand require great flexibility in the ways the hand and fingers are presented to the fingerboard. Perhaps the most thoughtful of these guitarists was Fernando Sor. The flexibility of left-hand positioning was an important part of Sor's technique. In his *Method for the Spanish Guitar,* published in London in 1830, he wrote: "The elbow, as I commonly place it, allows of being moved from or toward the body, according as the chord may require... Most passages that appear difficult, cease to have that appearance as soon as the elbow takes the proper position."[15] Sor later included this idea in his twelve maxims: "When it is necessary to give to the line of the ends of the fingers a direction parallel to the fret instead of the string, to make this change depend rather on the position of the elbow than on the motion of the wrist."[16]

Positioning of the Wrist

The **wrist** is the most complex joint of the upper limb.[17] It's construction allows a wide range of movement in flexion and extension and a limited side to side movement.

Wrist Alignment: The wrist contains a tunnel (the *carpal tunnel*) through which pass the tendons of the finger flexors and the median nerve (one of the three main nerves to the hand). The narrowness of this tunnel explains the frequent complaints guitarists have about nerve irritation. To decrease the potential of nerve problems, and to increase muscular efficiency, the alignment of both wrists with their forearms should be maintained at all times. There are instances where advanced guitarists let their right wrist deviate downward (toward the floor) from this position of alignment to facilitate certain techniques, but these deviations have little value unless the fingers are functioning effortlessly and problems of tone have been solved.

Arch of the Wrist: The positioning of the wrist of both hands should be important to guitarists. It has been called the "key joint of the hand."[18] The muscles and tendons of the fingers are not long enough to allow simultaneously maximum movements at the wrist and the fingers; complete flexion of the fingers is possible only if the wrist is in slight extension, and flexion of the wrist results in the automatic opening of the fingers.[19] Strain will result when muscles try to move joints that are positioned close to their limits of flexion or extension. Because finger flexion and extension are equally important to guitar playing (fingers must be able to release or extend comfortably before they can flex), the wrist must be positioned to allow the knuckle and middle joints of the fingers[20] to function close to their midrange position, between the comfortable limits of flexion and extension. This efficient midrange position allows the greatest freedom of movement in *both* directions. The arch (slight flexion) of the wrist determines the midrange position of the fingers. In right-hand technique the arch also determines where the thumb will contact the index finger: when the wrist is depressed (not quite fully extended), the tip of the thumb will contact the middle joint of the index finger; when the wrist is given a large arch (almost fully flexed), the thumb will pass under the fingers if it flexes. *Therefore, the wrist arch influences the positions of the thumb and fingers.*[21] For most guitarists, an effective arch will allow the tip of the thumb to follow-through against the tip joint of the index finger.

The Hand and Thumb

The five long bones found in the hand are the **metacarpals.** Although they are not usually referred to in guitar technique, the outer metacarpals, those for

15) Fernando Sor, *Method for the Spanish Guitar,* trans. A. Merrick (London: R. Cocks and Co., 1830; reprint, New York: Da Capo Press, 1971), 23.
16) Sor, 48.
17) Tubiana and Chamagne, 84.
18) Tubiana, 39.
19) Tubiana, 45.
20) There is no consistent terminology among guitarists for the names of the joints of the fingers. In this book the terms knuckle, middle, and tip will be used (Shearer, 30). The anatomical names for these joints are the metacarpal phalangeal joint (MP), proximal interphalangeal joint (PIP), and distal interphalangeal joint (DP).
21) Tubiana and Chamagne, 86.

the thumb and little finger, have much mobility. The thumb metacarpal is independent. The metacarpal for the little finger is semi-independent and has a range of movement of 20°.[22] There are many instances where movements of these metacarpals can significantly improve finger function. (See page 16.)

Movements of the Thumb

The **thumb** is an important finger because of its force, mobility, and ability to oppose to the other fingers.[23] The proper use of the thumb is important to the efficient development of right-hand technique; excess tension in the thumb can severely restrict the ability to control the positions and movements of the other fingers. Both Fernando Sor and Dionisio Aguado, compared to authors of more modern pedagogical works, introduced the thumb stroke before the introduction of right-hand finger strokes.[24]

The thumb contains the first metacarpal or wrist segment, middle segment, and tip segment. The nearer to the wrist these segments are, the more mobility they have. The joints controlling these segments are the wrist joint, middle joint, and tip joint.[25] Right-hand thumb strokes made from the wrist joint will activate the independent metacarpal which will allow greater freedom of movement and a greater reach. Extension from the middle joint of the thumb is almost nil.[26]

The Fingers

The abilities and limits of individual fingers and their joints need to be clearly understood to take full advantage of proper use. Fingers do not function identically. Further, the knuckle, middle, and tip joints are not of identical construction.

Most of the following observations are directed toward a better understanding of right-hand technique. Once the best position for the right hand and fingers has been developed, movement comes solely from the finger joints (except for string crossing and color changes). Left-hand positioning, as discussed earlier, is less static and often requires a wide range of positions and movements.

Many guitarists now speak of simple, economical, or efficient movements as if there is some universal understanding of what those things are. When these

things are defined, they may have the appearance and lure of sound principles, but may be true only in a superficial way. Ultimately they may impede true understanding. For example, the idea of an economical movement may sound efficient, but an economical movement is of no benefit unless it is the result of an economical effort. Many guitarists use great effort to make small movements.

The hand is complex, and what may appear to be a simple movement may actually cause a complex chain of events within the hand. There are two important facets of right-hand positioning and movement which should be thoroughly understood. Both have resulted in confusion and needless technical problems for guitarists. All hands contain some common "muscular dependencies." These occur when the position or movement of one finger or joint affects the free movement of another finger or joint. The most significant of these are the use of the tip joints in right-hand finger strokes and what is known as "The Quadrige Phenomenon." The use of the tip joints requires at least a superficial understanding of a complex subject: the way muscles act on a joint or joints, and sensitivity to the effects of the quadrige phenomenon is important for the refined positioning of the fingers in free stroke.

The Tip Joints

There is disagreement among guitarists about the use of the right-hand tip joints. Emilio Pujol, in his *Guitar School,* writes that one phase of rest stroke consists of "concentrating force into the fingertip and moving the string out of its position of equilibrium by means of a simple movement of the last joint towards the next adjacent string."[27] About free stroke he writes: "In this case, the finger will bend back on itself without even touching the next string, and will thus necessarily reduce the effort required by the resistance of the plucked string. In no case must this resistance be allowed to cause the last joint to yield in the opposite direction."[28]

Charles Duncan, in *The Art of Classical Guitar Playing,* writes: "Keep the tip-joints absolutely firm. Any joint collapse, no matter how small, can only slow the stroke."[29] He goes on to suggest that "it may help

22) Tubiana, 26.
23) Tubiana, 72.
24) Aaron Shearer's *Learning the Classic Guitar* is one modern method that begins with the thumb stroke.
25) The anatomical names for these joints are the trapezometacarpal joint (TM), metacarpal phalangeal joint (MP), and interphalangeal joint (IP).
26) Tubiana, 623.
27) Emilio Pujol, *Guitar School, A Theoretical-Practical Method for the Guitar, Books One & Two,* translated by Brian Jeffery, edited by Matanya Ophee, Editions Orphée, Boston, 1983, p. 56, 57.
28) Pujol, 57.
29) Charles Duncan, *The Art of Classical Guitar Playing,* (Princeton: Summy-Birchard Music, 1980), 76.

to think of the stroke as originating in an actual flex of the fingertip…"[30]

Aaron Shearer, in Part One of *Learning the Classic Guitar,* expresses a similar view: "Always maintain enough firmness in the tip joint to avoid its being displaced by the resistance of the string."[31] He then offers several advantages dealing with tone, security, and accuracy.

John Duarte, in *The Bases of Classic Guitar Technique,* writes about rest stroke: "…Ideally the fingertip should bend slightly under the growing pressure of the string, until it points directly down just before the string is released, since this prolongs the distance through which the string is pushed directly across, in the correct plane. In practice this can only be approximated, but many fine players do allow such *flexing* of the tip joint to occur during apoyando."[32] [Italics mine.] He is clearly recommending the tip joint yield slightly to the pressure of the string, but he refers to this as *flexing.* Flexion is a well defined muscular activity: it is the movement of a finger segment toward the palm of the hand. Duarte is evidently using the term in the sense of *flexible,* but this can lead to confusion.

Hector Quine, in *Guitar Technique,* maintains that "A theory which could be described as showing an *imperfect* understanding of the mechanics and physiology of right-hand finger action is that the tip joint should give way or 'flex' on contacting the string…"[33] [Italics mine.] Quine, like Duarte, also uses the term *flex* in an inappropriate way.

Pepe Romero writes this about the use of the tip joint in free stroke: "…each time a finger plays—touches the string, applies pressure and releases it—a small shock is produced. This shock must be absorbed by the flexibility of the distal interphalangeal [tip] joint, *which gives at the moment the initial pressure is being applied."[34]* [Italics mine.] In rest stroke he recommends the tip joint give slightly and then recover after the string is released.[35]

The authors advocating firm tip joints, or active and continuous flexion at the tip joint, apparently assume that the tip joint works the same as the middle and knuckle joints and that mechanical efficiency will be increased by its movement. As the following will show, continuous tension at the tip joint will have an adverse effect on the middle and knuckle joints. While advanced players may certainly play with varying degrees of tension in their tip joints, the best of them release it instantly. This ability to replace a muscular contraction with a relaxation is the foundation of effortless playing. Most beginners and intermediate students have not acquired the physical sensitivity to do this. Physical sensations can become contaminated and unreliable; they must become purified, through the reduction of tension, before they can become sensitive to the increase and release of minute gradations of tension. It is not surprising that advanced players may be unaware of this process within themselves.

Part of the problem may lie in the difficulty players and teachers have of watching the tip joints. These joints are usually hidden from view while the finger strokes a string, especially in free stroke. The tip joints may experience "passive flexion," as part of the middle joint follow-through, which may lead to the assumption that they have actively flexed while in contact with the string.

There are many muscles that power the movements of the fingers: nine extrinsic muscles (these are muscles in the forearm that send tendons out to the fingers) for the flexion and extension of the fingers; and nineteen intrinsic muscles (these are muscles in the hand itself) that contribute to the movement of the outer metacarpals and each finger segment.[36]

The effect these muscles have on joint movement is often complex. Although muscular contractions cause the flexion or extension of a joint, the result of their actions is not always limited to simple flexion or extension. Muscles can function as *agonist* or *antagonist.* Dr. Tubiana explains this concept: "It is important to realize that no muscle works alone. Muscles on opposite sides of a limb work like partners, and are called antagonists. Even the simplest movement requires the participation of antagonists. Movements are determined by the modulation of their respective forces. This is the essence of the important concept of 'synergistic antagonistic' forces."[37] Depending on their function as agonist or antagonist, muscles can do three things: (1) they can move a joint (simple contraction); (2) they can add to the stability of a joint (stabilizing contraction); (3) and they can exert a force that can actually interfere with a desired movement (unwanted

30) Duncan, 77.
31) Shearer, 59.
32) John Duarte, *The Bases of Classic Guitar Technique,* (Borough Green, Sevenoaks, Kent: Novello, 1975) 17.
33) Quine, 32.
34) Romero, 9.
35) Romero, 32.
36) Tubiana, 37.
37) Tubiana and Chamagne, 86.

contraction).[38] The last form of muscular contraction needs to be understood. These unwanted forces, which interfere with a desired movement, must be counterbalanced by opposing muscular forces which will lead to the application of further effort and increased tension. The attempt to develop independent movement of a joint under conditions where it is simply not possible will lead to frustration. No amount of force or effort will help. It will hinder progress. The ability to move a joint under these circumstances is not true independence.

Dr. René Malek, who has made a study of kinetic joint chains, explains the principles behind these effects: "The most obvious link between the joints in the same chain are the muscles acting *across two or more joints*. These are muscles which cross a number of joints without being inserted on the skeletal elements articulating at these joints. This is the case for almost all the muscles of the hand, particularly the extrinsic muscles such as the flexors and extensors. Their action is not limited to the mobilization of the joints on which they are inserted, but is also applied to the intervening joints."[39] Because the tip joint is the last joint of the finger, its tendons must cross the middle and knuckle joints and will influence those joints.

Dr. Malek describes the series of complex events when finger flexion begins with the tip joints (simplified and paraphrased here). When the tip joint is the first joint to flex, its segment is subjected to two different forces: the active force (agonist) applied by the *flexor digitorum profundus* and the stabilizing force (antagonist) applied by the *extensor digitorum profundus*. While the active force moves the tip segment, the stabilizing force exerts pressure on the head of the middle segment. As the movement proceeds, the knuckle segment is then subject to an extension force which is the sum of all the forces acting on the tip and middle segments. As the desired movement is flexion, these extension forces are counterproductive. To counterbalance these unwanted forces, other muscles and forces must be used.[40]

The force exerted on the knuckle segment can easily be seen with the following test: with the fingers close to their midrange position, quickly and forcefully flex the tip joints of all your fingers (the middle joints will move too). *The knuckle joints extend involuntarily*. There is also an extension force exerted at the middle joint. Although this force may not lead to movement, it will lead to muscular tension. Guitarists who play with rigid tip joints play with some of these unwanted forces but have learned to counter these forces with extra effort. This is a common cause of right hand tension. The problem beginners often have of extending their knuckles and pulling their fingers up as they stroke the string is not caused by misunderstanding the direction the finger should move; rather, it is caused by the tenseness of the tip joint which throws the knuckle joint into extension. Beginners have not yet learned how to counter this unwanted movement.

Electromyographic studies have discovered that from full extension of the fingers there is a specific sequence of flexion for the different joints of the fingers: the flexion of the fingers normally begins at the middle joint, followed by the knuckle and tip joints. The tip joint flexes more slowly than the middle joint, and its flexion is not completed until the end of the middle-joint movement.[41] *The efficient and comfortable flexion of the tip joint is thus dependent on the position of the middle joint.* From a flexed position, extension of the fingers begins at the knuckle joint, followed by the middle and tip joints.[42]

Because right-hand finger strokes usually start with the knuckle and middle joints of the fingers already positioned close to their midrange position with the fingertips just outside their strings, movement will usually start with the simultaneous flexion of the knuckle and middle joints. Again, if the tip joints are kept firm (trying to flex) throughout the stroke, unwanted and counterproductive forces will be exerted on the middle and knuckle joints.[43]

Continuous flexion of the tip joint throughout the stroke will also produce unwanted movements in the tips of adjacent fingers. Tip joint flexion will cause adjacent fingers to flex in sympathy. If an adjacent finger needs to extend, as in alternation, added effort will be required for this extension.

Right-hand training should proceed with an understanding of the following:

1) *Continuous flexion (tension) of the tip joint will impair the function of the other joints of the same finger.* Guitarists can learn to move their tip joints so they *appear* to be independent, but as shown above, true muscular independence is simply not possible.

---

38) Dr. Malek uses the terms simple, isometric, and parasitic for these contractions.
39) Tubiana, 218.
40) Tubiana, 220, 221.
41) Tubiana, 63.
42) Tubiana, 65.
43) Interestingly enough, these counterproductive forces are used to advantage when performing descending slurs: the flexion of the tip joint encourages extension from the knuckle.

Efficient and independent movement requires the application of minimum effort. This is accomplished through the elimination of extraneous and unneeded efforts through muscular contractions arising quickly and *immediately* being replaced by muscular relaxations. The finger segment then moves forward from this first muscular impulse. No added effort is required for the duration of the movement. The tip joints are not capable of this free follow-through or ballistic movement (see pages 18, 19 and 23).

Because the tip joints cannot comfortably and continuously flex until full flexion of the middle joint has occurred, the tip joints should not actively follow-through once the string has been sounded. Any effort to develop independent movement at the tip joint will lead to excessive tension and reduced independence in the other joints.

2) *Continuous flexion (tension) of the tip joint will result in the sympathetic flexion at the tip joints of adjacent fingers.* Again, guitarists can learn to prevent the *visible* effects of this sympathetic flexion, but unwanted muscular forces will still be there and must be countered.

It should be clear that many problems of excessive right-hand tension originate with the improper use of the tip joints. As mentioned above, it is not uncommon for sensations to become contaminated and unreliable—no amount of intellectual understanding or repositioning will cause a reduction of tension. What is needed is a way for the sensations to become purified and trustworthy again.

Beginners and remedial students will need to study right-hand finger strokes without the active participation of the tip joint. In both free stroke and rest stroke this means that the proper use of the tip joint requires that it gently yield to the resistance of the guitar string as the stroke is performed. In free stroke it will automatically spring back to its midrange position after the finger leaves the string. In rest stroke it returns to its midrange position as the finger begins its extension or release. The ability of the fingertip to clear the lower adjacent string in free stroke is determined by the angle of the middle joint (discussed below), not the flexion of the tip joint. This will enable students to learn to feel the benefits of the ballistic stroke (see page 23) and the release (see page 39).

Once the level of tension has been reduced, it will be appropriate to reintroduce some tension to the tip joint, but only if you can let go of it instantly. The test of this will be if you can still perform free and effortless finger movements. One of the properties of tension is that if we start at a place of minimal tension, we can increase tension by small increments. We cannot, however, start at a place of excessive tension and reduce it by small increments.[44]

The Middle Joint

The knuckle, middle, and tip joints each have different ranges of movements. The range of movement of the knuckle joint is about 85°, that of the middle joint about 115°, and that of the tip joint is about 80°.[45] (These numbers do vary slightly for each finger but are presented to show general relationships.) The middle joint, which has the widest range of movement (30° more than the knuckle joint), contributes to both rest stroke and free stroke and needs to be able to move comfortably for the finger to stroke the string. It should never be kept rigid.

In early free stroke training the angle at the middle joint should be adjusted toward the flexion side of the midrange, so the tip joint can yield to the resistance of the string and still clear the lower adjacent string. Advanced players who can effectively use their tip joints may have a slightly different position

The Knuckle Joint

The knuckle joint should never be kept immobile during right-hand finger movements. It moves in conjunction with the middle joint and is largely responsible for controlling the volume of attack. Volume (excluding considerations of tone quality—a fuller sound will also increase volume) is a result of the speed of the fingertip as it moves through the string and releases it. Because the knuckle joint is a more distant fulcrum, it will have a more efficient effect on the velocity of the fingertip than movement from the middle joint alone. This increase in velocity is not because the muscles for the knuckle joint are more powerful—they are not.[46] Movement from the knuckle joint will let the fingertip cover the distance needed for an efficient stroke in less time. The knuckle joints should be positioned so they can contribute some flexion *as the string is being sounded.* If the middle joint is the only joint moving the fingertip through the string, the dynamic range of the strokes will be limited.

44) See the explanation of Weber-Fechner Law of Physiology on pages 19 and 21.
45) Tubiana, 49.
46) This will come as a surprise to many guitarists who have simply assumed that the knuckle joints are the strongest joints.

The Quadrige Phenomenon

Several muscular dependencies are the result of the *phénomène du quadrige*[47] (four horse chariot). This phenomenon primarily affects the free movements of m and a in right-hand technique. When the a finger is fully extended and the m finger is flexed at the middle joint, the muscles lose all action on the tip joint of m. Free muscular movement at the middle joint is also significantly suppressed. The same phenomenon occurs when the little finger is fully extended and the a finger is flexed. (This effect can be eliminated by training the little finger to move in sympathy with the a finger.)

The main problem of cultivating effective movements of m and a (whether in arpeggios, tremolo, or scales) can be reduced through proper positioning. Right-hand formulae that include the a finger require that finger be positioned so the middle joint of m is unaffected by the quadrige phenomenon (any extension of a beyond the position of m will affect the tip joint of m), even if that means i and m must function on the flexion side of their midrange. As Aaron Shearer writes: "A finger can function with *more* flexion than it needs to clear an adjacent string, but it can't function with *less.*"[48]

The Index Finger

The flexors and extensors of the index finger are, in most cases, independent. This independence in both flexion and extension accounts for the heavy use this finger gets in right-hand technique. Preferred right-hand patterns for scale playing and other textures are those taking advantage of an alternation of the index with another finger: i-m and i-a (or m-i and a-i), or p-i. Arpeggio patterns requiring opposed motion (alternation) between the fingers are easier if the opposition (where needed and possible) can occur between the index and another finger. But the index finger has less flexion at the knuckle joint than the other fingers, because it opposes the thumb.[49] Guitarists should not force the follow-through of this finger to make it "look like" the others.

The index finger also has independence in *abduction* and *adduction* (the ability to move from side to side). This independence (along with its independence in extension) can be of great advantage in left-hand technique: when difficult reaches are needed between the first and fourth fingers, a different presentation of the hand to the fingerboard (dynamic positioning) may allow the reach to be taken with the first finger while the fourth finger maintains its midrange position. Because of the index finger's independence in extension, many difficult chord shapes can be more accessible if you position the highest finger first (usually the fourth finger) followed successively by lower fingers (the third, second, and first).

The Middle Finger

This finger has limited independence in both flexion and extension, primarily from its dependence on the ring finger for comfortable movement (a result of the quadrige effect). This dependence can be reduced in an i-m alternation by training the ring and little finger to move freely with m. The middle finger does have more strength in flexion than the index finger.[50] This may be why some guitarists prefer to play scales with m-i as opposed to i-m.

The Ring Finger

The arrangement of tendons (quadrige phenomenon) explains the dependence this finger has on the middle and little fingers for flexion and extension. Great care should be taken to insure that this finger is positioned in its best position. Guitarists can increase the mobility of the ring finger of the right hand by moving the little finger with it in sympathy.

The Little Finger

This finger has about half the strength of the middle finger in flexion. It does have its own musculature, and should be capable of independence, but these muscles only activate the metacarpal and the knuckle segment. For many guitarists, the position of the left hand puts the knuckle joint of this finger at its limit of extension, making further extension difficult. Adjusting the arch of the left wrist, so the finger joints are close to their midrange position, will let guitarists gain control of the knuckle joint and reinforce its movement with the metacarpal.

Although not commonly addressed in right-hand technique, control of this finger is essential; its movements, or lack of them, will influence the ring and middle fingers. Extension of the little finger inhibits the flexion of m and $a;$ and flexion at the middle and

---

47) Tubiana, 391.
48) Shearer, 72.
49) Tubiana, 50.
50) Tubiana, 73.

tip joints of the little finger results in sympathetic flexion at the middle and tip joints of the m and a. The relaxed control of this finger will allow m and a to work more effectively. Attention directed to the relaxation of the tip of the little finger will also increase the control of these fingers.

Anatomical Variations of the Hand • • • • • • • • • • • • • • •

Although technical principles grow out of the physiological similarities among individuals, there are several deviations from the "anatomical norm." The more common of these variations (those dealing with the length and proportion of the fingers) will be found in guitarists at all levels of development. The rarer variants (those dealing with extra interconnections between the tendons of the fingers and thumb, or the absence of certain muscles or tendons) may prevent technical proficiency from developing beyond a rudimentary level. Although teachers of advanced students may never see these problems, teachers of beginners should be aware of these possibilities. Often what may be perceived as inability may be the result of a physiological variation.

Proportion of Finger Segments

There are ideal proportions between the lengths of fingers and the size of the bones making up the fingers. The metacarpal and three segments of each finger form a chain of precise relationships: the length of the metacarpal and segments of the same finger correspond to the Fibonacci series (0, 1, 1, 2, 3, 5, 8, 13, etc.). This series of numbers, devised by Leonardo Fibonacci, a Thirteenth-Century Italian mathematician, derives each number by adding together the two previous numbers. The length of the metacarpal segment is equal to the sum of the lengths of the knuckle and middle segments; the length of knuckle segment is equal to the lengths of the middle and tip segments. The series corresponds to an "equiangular spiral." Biologists have recognized that this typical progression corresponds to the natural biologic spirals found in other forms of life, like flowers and sea shells.[51]

Length of Fingers

The knuckle and middle segments of the middle and ring fingers are longer than those of the index finger.[52] The middle finger, and usually the ring finger, are longer than the index finger. When the fingers are extended and separated, the tips of the fingers lie on the circumference of a circle whose center is the head of the third metacarpal.[53] (This is beneath the middle finger.)

Students with an excessively long middle finger, or short index finger, may benefit from cultivating an i-a or a-i alternation as their standard right-hand scale fingering.

Other Variations

There is another category of anatomical variation that is not immediately visible; these variations have to do with the presence of extra connecting tendons or the absence of certain muscles or tendons. Some of the more common are explained below.

1) In a small percentage of people, one or more intertendinous connections can exist between the thumb and the index finger. This extra connection restricts independence between the thumb and index finger.[54] This interdependent flexion of the tip joints of the thumb and index occurs in about 1 in 200 cases.[55]

2) The extrinsic muscles of the index finger are usually independent. In about 10% of cases, this independence of flexion is limited by connections that will force the index finger into interdependent actions with the middle, ring, and little fingers at the tip joints.[56]

3) About 15% of the general population does not have an independent flexor tendon for the middle joint of the little finger. This tendon allows independent flexion of the little finger at the middle joint.[57]

4) The *palmaris longus* (wrist flexor) is absent in 10% to 13% of the general population.

51) Tubiana, 48.
52) Tubiana and Chamagne, 84.
53) Tubiana, 21.
54) H. Kirk Watson, M.D. and Rami Kalus, M.D. "Achieving Independent Finger Flexion—The Guitarist's Advantage," *Medical Problems of Performing Artists,* Vol. 2, No. 2, June 1987, 59.
55) Watson and Kalus, 59.
56) Raoul Tubiana, M.D., "Functional Anatomy of the Hand," *Medical Problems of Performing Artists,* Vol. 3, No. 4, December 1988, 126.
57) Watson and Kalus, 58.

Developing Technical Ability · ·

Because "movements, not muscles, are represented in the cerebral cortex,"[58] it is not necessary (or perhaps even possible) to understand which muscles control which joints. It has become clear to physiologists that many muscles are used in the production of even a simple movement.[59] Yet it is important to cultivate a general understanding of how muscles act on a joint. This can lead to the knowledge of how to use a joint more effectively. Once correctly patterned habits of movement are established, technique can develop rapidly. Speed, power, and ease of movement are the result of timing and coordination. The common admonition to "play relaxed" misses the point—a relaxed quality is the result of good technique, not the cause.

Technique is more than speed and power—it is the sum of all the skillful movements needed to make music—from a rapid *forte* scale to a delicate chord voicing. The main concern in early technical training should be the positioning of the body so it can respond more efficiently to the commands of the brain. The next concern is to move the fingers in such a way to take advantage of this efficiency.

George Kochevitsky, in *The Art of Piano Playing,* describes a study which determined the speed of individual finger repetitions. This study showed "that on the average a person could make from five to six movements a second with the second and third fingers [index and middle] and from four to five movements a second with each of the other fingers."[60] Although practicing with the intent of increasing the agility of individual fingers may be worthless, it is not worthless to study the movements of individual fingers to try to refine the timing and coordination of their joints, and to develop a sensitivity to the efficient contraction and relaxation of muscles. Dr. Frank R. Wilson writes:

> Slow practice is the key to rapid technical progress. The cerebellum is a non-judgmental part of the brain; it assumes that any repetitive activity in the muscular system is being repeated because the conscious mind is trying to make it automatic. The cerebellum will be just as efficient automatizer of incorrect sequences of timing as those that are correct. When practicing takes place at a pace too fast for accurate playing, there is little chance for the material to be mastered,

and reliable, confident performance simply will not occur. On the other hand, it is probably true that practice for speed is seldom necessary. The cerebellum can supply all the speed wanted *if patterning is correct during practice.[61]* [Italics mine.]

The purpose of this important slow practice should be to insure that the positions and movements are the best they can be. Practice that includes the mindless repetition of movements without a sense of purpose is useless. These gymnastics, although of comfort to the unimaginative guitarist, will not lead to efficient progress. The real value of technical exercises is the opportunity they give us to respond and adapt to a series of increasingly difficult challenges. These increasingly difficult technical environments will call for more sensitivity and control for our hands to be able to function effectively.

Kochevitsky describes this process:

> Suppose we are performing a new motor act (that is, beginning to form a conditioned reflex). Then the nervous process taking its course the first time irradiates not only over the immediate surroundings of the stimulated center along the path of temporary connections. It also irradiates considerably through the motor centers of the cortex, exciting various points of this region. It is manifested in many unnecessary movements and needless muscle contractions.[62]
>
> The execution of a complex movement requires not only precise timing regulation but also the involvement of the *least muscle work needed for any given action.* [Italics mine.] This is achieved by localizing the excitatory process.[63]
>
> Through practice we can learn to move our fingers at the right time and in exact succession in accordance with a given musical figure… *The elimination of too much muscle action is the real basis for developing agility.[64]* [Italics mine.]

This gives us some insight into the awkwardness, fatigue, and clumsiness beginners experience if they proceed to tasks for which the muscles and the mind are not prepared. The problem of technical velocity lies in the flexibility of the central nervous system and, in Kochevitsky's words, "the dexterity of the mind."[65]

It is the resilience of the central nervous system and the brain that allows great virtuosos to quickly replace muscular contractions with muscular relaxations. This is the final element needed to develop correct patterns of movement. Muscles move a joint by contracting. These contractions must arise quickly, last a short time, and alternate with relaxations. Be-

---

58) Tubiana and Chamagne, 86.
59) Tubiana, 219.
60) George Kochevitsky, *The Art of Piano Playing,* (Princeton: Summy-Birchard Music, 1967), 12.
61) Frank R. Wilson, M.D., *Mind, Muscle and Music,* (Elkhart: The Selmer Company), 14.
62) Kochevitsky, 27.
63) Kochevitsky, 26.
64) Kochevitsky, 13.
65) Kochevitsky, 41.

sides providing muscular freedom to the muscles and a release of tension, this process also allows for increased coordination between muscles that must work together or in sequence. This is especially important for fingers that must abruptly change direction from flexion to extension.

Dr. Wilson gives us some information about this important discovery:

The first important clue to understanding the control of these movements was discovered almost ninety years ago. In 1895, Paul Richer took a series of rapid-sequence photographs of the quadriceps muscle during a kicking motion. After studying the photographs, he said this about the contraction of the muscle during the kick: 'It is very energetic and short lasting. It launches the limb in a set direction and ceases long before the limb will have completed its course of action. Because of the similarity of this kind of move to the firing of a gun shell, it was called 'ballistic.'

It is now recognized that highly skilled movements, particularly those that are rapidly executed and brief in duration, are under the guidance of a far more complex control system than is required for movements which can be corrected by ongoing adjustment, or so-called current control. It must be emphasized that the movements themselves need not be shot-like to come under the ballistic mode of control. The essential characteristic of the control system is that *the details of the movement must have been completely worked out in advance*, in a lengthy trial and error process, so that the movements can be executed when called for with absolute accuracy, each and every time in an automatic way. This means that the brain, to the motor control system, must issue in advance of the move an ordered series of command signals that specify what the muscles involved must do, from start to finish, before the movement itself actually begins. *Since there is no time to correct mistakes once the move has begun, everything must be right from the very beginning.*[66] [Italics mine.]

Practicing ● ● ● ● ● ● ● ● ● ● ● ● ● ● ● ● ● ●

Practice is, among other things, the process of working out the precise details of movements beforehand. The purpose of practice is to improve the ability to perform. The application of sound technical principles contributes to the development and refinement of the technical freedom needed to perform music at the highest level.

One popular approach to developing technical ability advocates the application of increasing levels of force and effort to overcome difficulties. The use of will power can get some impressive short term results and can compensate for technical deficiencies—but

with a price. Force not converted into movement does not simply disappear; this excess force turns into tension which creates unneeded heat and friction in the joints. The resulting stresses on the muscles and joints can actually damage the technical mechanism. Because there is a limit to the force that can be applied to any task, there will be a limit to improvement. Over a period of time technical ability may begin to deteriorate.

A contrasting approach seeks to increase sensitivity to tension and movement to help reduce the muscular effort needed to play the guitar. Because there is no limit to the sensitivity we can acquire, there will be no limit to improvement. This approach cultivates light, effortless, and well organized movements. Anat Baniel, a well known teacher of the Feldenkrais Method, says: "…in a well-organized movement, the forces generated by muscular contractions are translated into movement or into pressure exerted on an external object."[67] Yochanan Rywerant, author of *The Feldenkrais Method: Teaching by Handling,* describes the process of developing more efficient and easier movements:

1. From the functional point of view, mere repetition involves going through, again and again, the same well-known pattern. Improvement, however, involves something quite different: a change in our patterns of functioning.

2. Conscious change of a pattern inevitably means learning: discerning and distinguishing between several possible patterns of movement or action, appreciating small differences and details, and being able to choose and act on those various possibilities.

3. To be able to discern minute differences in muscular patterns there must be a diminution in the overall proprioceptive[68] sensory excitation—*muscular effort must be cut to a minimum.* [Italics mine.] This is in accordance with the well-known Weber-Fechner law in physiology, which holds that the threshold of sensitivity to changes in sensory excitation is a certain fraction of the overall excitation already present.

4. The use of will power (effort) implies, psychologically, the juxtaposition of one's present level of performance against an ideal goal not yet achieved. Obviously, the repetition of the same pattern means that subsequent repetitions promise little improvement. One is therefore frustrated, and this frustration, combined with a reinforced expectation of failure, may easily lead to a state of anxiety.

5. Neurologically, the repetition of a particular pattern of movement creates a well-trodden pathway along which efferent impulses may pass through the relevant synapses. This repetition diminishes the likelihood of alternative patterns arising; the one pattern becomes compulsive and so within the context of a certain activity there is no other possibility.[69]

---

66) Frank R. Wilson, *Tone Deaf and All Thumbs?*, 49-50.
67) Mary Spire, M.A., "The Feldenkrais Method: An Interview with Anat Baniel," *Medical Problems of Performing Artists,* Vol. 4, No. 4, December 1989, 159.
68) Sensations from movements of parts of the body which are conveyed to the central nervous system are called "proprioceptive" (self-perceiving), the ability to feel how one moves.
69) Yochanan Rywerant, *The Feldenkrais Method: Teaching by Handling,* (San Francisco: Harper & Row, 1983), 214-216.

This "well-trodden pathway" is a result of the neurophysiologic Law of Facilitation: once a nerve impulse or stimulus has traveled through a specific route, it is easier for the next impulse to make the same passage. For all succeeding impulses, the passage will be even easier. This law is simply a neurophysiological explanation of habit.

The following, freely drawn from Moshe Feldenkrais' *Awareness Through Movement,* can provide a framework within which the technical principles presented later can be applied:

1. Improvement means change.

Change happens through choices based on our increased sensitivity to movement and tension, and our awareness of proper use.

2. Observation of the self is better than mechanical repetition.

Feldenkrais writes:

> …all methods of gymnastics are based on the repetition of action. And not only gymnastics—everything we learn is based largely on the principle of repetition and committing to memory. This may make it easy to understand why one man may practice daily on a musical instrument and fail to make any progress, while another shows daily improvement. Perhaps the nature of the talent that is the accepted explanation for this divergence of achievement derives from the fact the second student observes what he is doing while he plays while the first one only repeats and memorizes and relies on the assumption that sufficient repetition of a bad performance will somehow bring about musical perfection.[70]

3. Performance is improved by the separation of the aim from the means.

This is especially difficult for music students to understand. The aim of their study is to play pieces and to develop as artists. But if the means to these aims are not adequately developed, failure and frustration will result. The quality of the means will determine the quality of the end.

> A too-strong wish for the aim often causes internal tension. This tension not only hinders your achieving the desired aim, but may even endanger life—as, for instance, in crossing a road, when the aim is at all costs to catch a bus on the other side and attention is diverted completely from the surroundings.[71]

> In most cases where an action is linked to a strong desire,

the efficiency of the action may be improved by separating the aim from the means of achieving it. A motorist in a desperate hurry to reach his destination, for instance, will fare better if he entrusts the wheel to a man who is a good driver but not desperate to reach the destination in time.[72]

It is important, though, not to forget the aim of study: it should merely be placed in the background. A musician who forgets the aim of his work, concentrating only on the means, will lose interest and become bored or practice some meaningless mechanical activity. One important role of the teacher is to know the final goals and to see that the student's focus on the means will lead to those goals.

4. Increase your ability, not your effort.

This is remarkably similar to Fernando Sor's second maxim from his *Method for the Spanish Guitar:* "To require more from *skill* than from *strength.*"[73] This is done through the observation of the self:

> To the extent that ability increases, the need for conscious efforts of the will decreases. The effort required to increase ability provides sufficient and efficient exercise for our will power… People who know how to operate effectively do so without great preparation and without much fuss. Men of great will power tend to apply too much force instead of using moderate forces more effectively.

> If you rely on your will power, you will develop your ability to strain and become accustomed to applying an enormous amount of force to actions that can be carried out with much less energy, if it is properly directed and graduated.[74]

5. To understand movement, we must feel, not strain.

> To learn we need time, attention, and discrimination; to discriminate we must sense. This means that in order to learn we must sharpen our powers of sensing, and if we try to do most things by sheer force we shall achieve precisely the opposite of what we need…

> When learning is carried out under conditions of maximum effort, and even this does not seem enough, there is no longer any way of speeding up action or making it stronger or better, because the individual has already reached the limit of his capacity.[75]

> …in order to recognize small changes in effort, the effort itself must first be reduced. More delicate and improved control of movement is possible only through the increase of sensitivity, through a greater ability to sense differences.[76]

70) Moshe Feldenkrais, *Awareness Through Movement,* (New York: Harper & Row, 1972), 137.
71) Feldenkrais, 82.
72) Feldenkrais, 82.
73) Sor, 48.
74) Feldenkrais, 59.
75) Feldenkrais, 58-59.
76) Feldenkrais, 58-59.

If you are in a room with one hundred lit candles, you won't notice if one more is added. But if there are only three candles, you can easily tell when a fourth is lit. This is an illustration of the Weber-Fechner law in physiology referred to earlier. The candles represent tension, or force. If you are straining with exertion you won't be sensitive to the subtle messages your body sends. Nor will you be sensitive to the subtle musical refinements which result from minute variations of force or pressure. Over stimulation can mask sensation.

6. Effective action improves the body and its capacity to act.

The effectiveness of an action is judged first of all by the simple standard of whether it achieves its purpose. But that test is not sufficient. Action must also improve a living and developing body at least to the extent that the same action will be carried out more effectively the next time.[77]

The advice commonly given students that "whatever works must be right" is usually presented with the prosaic rationale that "it seems to get the job done." Getting the job done, though, isn't enough: beginners, and often their teachers, may not have a proper appreciation of what the job is. As players become more advanced, their understanding of the "job description" grows and the requirements they make of their technique grow. The job expands from just hitting the notes to investing them with a meaningful musical presence while maintaining an effortless technique.

7. There is no limit to improvement.

Every time that we expand the limits of our knowledge, our sensibility and the precision of our actions increase and the limits of what is considered natural and normal also expand.

The more an individual advances his development the greater will be his ease of action, the ease synonymous with harmonious organization of the senses and the muscles. When activity is freed of tension and superfluous effort the resulting ease makes for greater sensitivity and better discrimination, which make for still greater ease in action. He will now be able to identify unnecessary effort in actions that formerly seemed easy to him. As this sensitivity in action is further refined, it continues to become increasingly delicate up to a certain level.[78]

This is good news for all students of the guitar. Practicing is the act of recognizing all our unclaimed possibilities, and then claiming them through the increasingly effective use of ourselves.

Technical Principles ·········

Six important principles dealing with the positioning and movement of our bodies can be distilled from the previous discussions.[79] These principles can apply to all guitarists, but their intelligent application should take account of the differences among individuals.

Kochevitsky writes:

All human beings are subject to the same physiological laws, all normal human bodies are built on identical principles: they have similar skeletal construction, muscle function, similarly working central nervous systems. They are at least similar to such a degree that it is possible to speak of common physiological laws governing motor activity—hence the common prerequisites for building the foundation of a piano technique.[80]

The purpose and use of these principles need to be understood. The discoveries of F.M. Alexander, whose important work was mentioned earlier, were not limited to what constituted proper use. Alexander found that when he tried to change the use of himself, the stimulus to misuse himself was much stronger than his ability to change. He relied on "what felt right" which was conditioned by past habits.[81]

Michael Gelb, in his book *Body Learning,* quotes Alexander on this subject:

I was indeed suffering from the delusion that is practically universal, the delusion that because we are able to do what we 'will to do' in acts that are habitual and involve familiar sensory experiences, we shall be equally successful in doing what we 'will to do' in acts which are contrary to our habit and therefore involve sensory experiences that are unfamiliar.[82]

Nikolaas Tinbergen, Professor of Animal Behavior at Oxford and recipient of the 1973 Nobel Prize for Physiology or Medicine, devoted most of his Nobel Lecture to Alexander's work. He explains Alexander's key discoveries:

There are many strong indications that, at various levels of integration, from single muscle units up to complex behavior, the correct performance of many movements is continuously checked by the brain. It does this by comparing a feedback report that says 'orders carried out' with the feedback expectation for which, with the initiation of each movement, the brain has been alerted. Only when the expected feedback and the actual feedback match does the brain stop sending out

77) Feldenkrais, 85.
78) Feldenkrais, 87.
79) The alignment and midrange principles owe a debt to Aaron Shearer's work. See Shearer, 10.
80) Kochevitsky, 37.
81) Michael Gelb, *Body Learning,* (New York, Henry Holt and Company, 1987), 12.
82) Gelb, 12.

commands for corrective action. Already the discoverers of this principle, Von Holst and Mittlestaedt, knew that the functioning of this complex mechanism could vary from moment to moment with the internal state of the subject... But what Alexander has discovered beyond this is that a lifelong misuse of the body muscles (such as caused by too much sitting and too little walking) can make the entire system go wrong. As a consequence, reports that 'all is correct' are received by the brain (or perhaps interpreted as correct) *when in fact all is very wrong.*[83] [Italics mine.]

In other words, our feelings are not reliable when we try to change our habits of positioning and movement when those habits are the result of misuse. But, as Alexander reasoned, "Surely if it is possible for feeling to become untrustworthy as a means of direction, it should also be possible to make it trustworthy again."[84] This is done by freeing ourselves from our dependence on "what feels right" and cultivating the ability to rely on conscious reasoning and observation. As new habits are developed, our sense of "what feels right" will emerge as a reliable guide. The following principles can give this process clarity and direction...

Principles of Positioning

Alignment: The most beneficial functioning of muscles requires they be aligned with the joints they control. Nerves should be aligned with the areas they supply. The spinal column should be aligned with the neck and head. This will increase the muscular efficiency and reduce the potential of nerve impingement.

A proper seating position will preserve the alignment of the back, neck, and head. Proper positioning of the left and right hands with their forearms will preserve the alignment of the flexor and extensor muscles and tendons with their joints.

Midrange Position: Speed and ease of playing on the guitar are a function of the efficient use of both the extensor and the flexor muscles. The finger joints of both hands should be positioned as close as possible to their powerful and efficient midrange position, so they can move comfortably and freely in both directions. What is often overlooked is that this midrange position of the fingers depends on the flexion (arch) of the wrist. Thus, the wrist should be arched so the knuckle and middle joints fall in their midrange position, at least as a point of departure.

Dynamic Positioning: Advanced technique often requires a change, or series of changes, in the way the hands are presented to the instrument while preserving the most efficient positions of the wrist and fingers.

These changes are usually best achieved by manipulating the larger and more mobile joints of the arm to affect the presentation of the hands and fingers. This applies to the use of movements from the shoulder to shift the left hand up, down, and across the fingerboard and to a slight rotation of the forearm, often in conjunction with movement of the left elbow toward or away from the body (this movement actually starts from the shoulder), to place the left hand in the best position for reaching certain chords or notes while maintaining a mechanically advantageous position of the finger joints. The effect of these movements on the fingers is often underestimated.

Application of this principle to right-hand technique requires movements be made from the shoulder to allow the right wrist and fingers to preserve their alignment and midrange position while crossing strings. Movement from the elbow will naturally accompany this movement.

Principles of Movement

Many of the different schools of guitar technique identify themselves by the positions they advocate. Although important and easily seen, these differences of positioning cannot give students all the information they need. The positioning of the body is important only so far as it allows or prevents certain beneficial things from taking place inside the body. These beneficial things are impossible to see directly and may be impossible to describe. Because of their elusive and subjective nature, it is difficult to adequately transform physical sensations into words. The following principles of movement try to describe some of the requirements of effortless movement.

Sequence, Range, and Direction of Joint Movement: The flexion of the right-hand fingers should consist of a combined movement from the knuckle and middle joints to bring the finger to the string and to follow-through. The tip joints should not be under continuous active tension.

The middle joint, which has a wider range of movement than the other finger joints, should have a significant participation in the stroke. This is true for both rest stroke and free stroke, though in rest stroke the action of the middle joint is reduced because its movement is stopped by the next lower string. The timing and balance between these two joints adds to technical fluency. Release of the finger begins at the knuckle joint followed by the middle joint.

---

83) Nikolaas Tinbergen, "Ethology and Stress Diseases," *Journal of Research in Singing,* Volume 5, No. 1, December 1981.
84) Gelb, 13.

Invariably, the knuckle and middle joints of the same finger should move in the same direction. The simultaneous flexion at one joint and extension at another quickly leads to fatigue and a loss of coordination. The flexibility of the tip joint while the middle joint is flexing is not opposed motion: the middle and tip joints are incapable of opposition.[85] As shown earlier, continuous tension at the tip joint will actually cause opposed muscular impulses which must be overcome.

The left-hand fingers, when extending and flexing, will move primarily from their knuckle joints. The tip joints will passively preserve their midrange position, except in descending slurs.

Economy of Muscular Effort: Through slow, directed practice, superior coordination can be developed as the impulse from the brain learns to excite only the muscles needed for the successful execution of a given movement, and to give those muscles minimum stimulation. This will eliminate needless movements and muscle contractions. The result of these economical impulses is an apparent "economy of movement." *But these economical movements are the result of refined muscular activity, not the cause.* Do not try to limit the size of finger movements by "putting on the brakes" with the opposing muscle group. The simultaneous contraction of flexors and extensors on a joint is a major cause of tension and inefficiency.

Ballistic Movement: Muscular contractions arise quickly and launch a finger segment through its movement. Once the movement has begun, the muscle relaxes and the inertia of the contraction allows the segment to follow-through on its own. This follow-through should be neither inhibited nor exaggerated—

both introduce added and unneeded muscle contractions. The strength of the initial contraction will determine the speed and amount of finger movement. Efficiency in extension can be achieved by simply allowing the finger to return to its midrange position. If proper positioning has been maintained, little effort will be needed. These technical refinements, perhaps more than any others, are responsible for the effortless quality superior players bring to their playing. But because there is no opportunity to correct mistakes once a movement has begun, the correct patterning of a movement has to be worked out and established earlier through careful practice. The ability of the central nervous system to quickly and continuously alternate muscular contractions with relaxations is the true cause of technical fluency.

The follow-through is the result of the muscular freedom caused by the economical effort and ballistic principles. A follow-through will not necessarily cause muscular freedom. Aaron Shearer's definition of the follow-through principle states: "Muscles function most efficiently only when there is sufficient follow-through to avoid a buildup of counterproductive tension. Sufficient follow-through means that, once a movement has been initiated, no intentional restraint is applied to the movement."[86] But if the follow-through is performed while applying more muscular force during the movement in an attempt to move the finger more or faster, too much effort will be exerted and muscular freedom will not develop. The follow-through itself is no guarantee that muscles are functioning most efficiently.

85) Tubiana, 60.
86) Shearer, 10.

Conclusion

The often repeated statement of established artists that "technique is developed through the music" is as true as it is misleading. Superior technique develops and grows from the demands imposed by a highly trained and musical ear. The ear demands to hear connections between notes others might not notice; it demands the technical freedom to push a musical phrase forward to heighten the tension; it demands to hear the utmost clarity and brilliance in a rapid scale passage. Ultimately, it demands to have its musical desires satisfied and the technique (the way we use ourselves) must be free to satisfy those demands.

Beginning students often interpret this statement of the mature artist as "technique is *created* by playing pieces." But without the discipline of a secure technical and musical foundation, artistic freedom will not develop. The artist's ability to interpret the literature on the highest level is the result of discipline and creativity.

The attempted movement toward technical fluency and artistic wisdom can best be described as a journey. It is a journey we can make only through continuous exploration, self-evaluation, and discovery. This journey may take many shapes: for some, it will be a circle leading nowhere; for others it will feel like a confusing and frustrating maze; and still others will feel trapped in a box. But the most liberating journey is the one that allows you to move along an ever ascending spiral. It is my hope that this book allows you to break free and begin the movement along this spiral.

There is a lot to assimilate here. I recommend that you restudy the difficult factual material as you pass through higher and higher levels of understanding. These new levels of understanding may allow you to process these facts into more meaningful knowledge, and to creatively apply that knowledge to your study of the guitar.

Lesson One

Seating

Seating and positioning the guitar have two aims: the guitar needs to be held comfortably and securely, and the hands must have free access to the entire range of the fingerboard (left hand) and all six strings (right hand). But the terms "comfortable" and "free" are subjective. Many guitarists insist they are comfortable when it is evident they have merely developed a tolerance for muscular tension. They are unaware of this excess tension because they have never felt the absence of tension.

The principle of alignment can help you objectively evaluate your seating position.

The application of this principle to a mechanically advantageous seating position lies in the alignment of the muscles of the back, neck, and shoulders. The shoulders should remain horizontal, even when playing in the upper positions. The neck should be positioned as an extension of the spine and should not be bent forward or turned sharply to the left to watch the hands. The resulting distanced view of the hands can be a great asset in advanced playing—changes of position can be followed by a slight movement of the eyes, rather than by movements of the neck and head.

Once this alignment has been obtained, the guitar should then be positioned respecting the body. If this position can be kept while playing, the hands will have easy and comfortable access to the entire range of the fingerboard and all six strings. You should not, as is often recommended, first put the left foot on a footstool, place the guitar on the left thigh, and then manipulate the torso to accommodate the instrument. The lower back should not collapse, and the shoulders should not drop to bring the hands and arms closer to the instrument. The torso should not lean to the left to ease playing in the upper positions, and the neck should not bend down and turn sharply to the left to watch the fingerboard.

Many of the old masters were aware of these problems, either intuitively or analytically, and offered well defined solutions. Dionisio Aguado (1784-1849) in his *New Guitar Method,* first published in Madrid in 1843, described the invention of a tripod on which the guitar was fixed. The height and angle of the guitar could be adjusted without changing the guitarist's position to allow one to obtain a position that is "natural and graceful."[87] Aguado later offered some specific advice: "The player's posture should be natural; the body should be held straight, without slumping as if to peer forward, or leaning to the left as beginners generally do… The base of the neck [of the guitar] should be slightly to left of the midline of the body, since the left hand thus remains free to reach all the frets without more support than the strength of the wrist, and does not depend on support from the body. The angle of the neck [of the guitar] must be such that the left hand can cover the fingerboard comfortably from end to end, without tiring when the first frets are used, and without difficulty when the rest are played."[88] An illustration of Aguado shows him to be in an excellent position relative to the guitar: the back muscles are aligned, the shoulders are horizontal, and the left arm appears to have easy access to the entire range of the fingerboard.

87) Dionisio Aguado, *New Guitar Method,* ed. Bryan Jeffery, trans. Louise Bigwood (London: Tecla, 1981), 7.
88) Aguado, 14-15.

Figure 1: Dionisio Aguado from his *New Guitar Method*

Fernando Sor (1778-1839) approached the problem differently, although his results were similar. In his *Method for the Spanish Guitar* he wrote: "Having had no master, I have been obliged to reason before raising any maxim into a fixed principle. I observed that all masters on the pianoforte agree in sitting opposite the middle of the keyboard, namely the middle of the horizontal line passed over by both hands. I considered this precept very just, because, leaving both arms equally separated from the body, no motion would be confined. Hence I concluded that the middle part of the string (the 12th fret) should be found opposite my body."[89] Sor presented an unorthodox way of positioning the guitar: an illustration accompanying his text shows the upper right bout of the instrument supported by a table![90] Yet the guitar itself is in a position very similar to that of Aguado's.

Figure 2: Fernando Sor from his *Method for the Spanish Guitar*

89) Sor, 10.
90) This unusual advice could be a remnant of certain schools of lute playing. Thomas Mace in *Musick's Monument* (1676) describes a seating position for the lute using a table, (Paris, Editions du Cente National de le Recherch Scientifique, 1966), 71.Thomas Robinson suggests the same in his *Schoole of Musicke* (London, 1603; reprint, New York: Da Capo Press, 1973).

Seating Procedure

The uninformed use of the standard footstool may be responsible for more technical problems than most guitarists are aware. If the footstool is too low, students compensate by leaning to the left or dropping their shoulders to bring their hands to the instrument. If the footstool is too high, the extreme position of the left leg may, over the years, cause serious damage to the nerves in the lower back.

There are other choices. Some guitarists now use special mechanical devices or cushions to help elevate the guitar. These methods allow the option of sitting all the way back on the chair for extra support while keeping both feet on the floor. The most versatile of these is the Guitar A-Frame Support. The Guitar A-Frame Support offers great flexibility in positioning the guitar to the body.[91] (Students who wish to use the footstool should follow Aaron Shearer's procedure in *Learning the Classic Guitar, Part One.*[92])

1) Sit comfortably on the chair. You may sit forward on the front edge or all the way back so the back of the chair can support your lower back. Allow your spine to lengthen and your shoulders widen without holding your back rigid. Raise your neck and head as though they were an extension of your spine.

2) Attach the Guitar A-Frame Support to the guitar and position the strap on your left thigh. Allow your legs to release away from your pelvis. This will allow room for the lower bout of the guitar. Some guitarists prefer to sit a little toward the right side of the chair so the positioning of their right leg is not hampered by the right front leg of the chair.

3) Make any needed adjustments to the placement of the upper suction cups so the upper left bout of the guitar rests slightly to the right of the center of your chest. The base of the neck of the guitar rests slightly to the left of the midline of the body as recommended by Aguado. Although Sor simply said the 12th fret should be found opposite the body, his illustration clearly shows the 12th fret positioned to the left of the midline of the body. The Nineteenth-Century guitar had a smaller body and shorter string length than the modern guitar.

4) Hold the guitar in position by lightly placing the underside of the right forearm on the top of the guitar at the lower bout so the fingers fall a little to the right of the soundhole. Some students will contact the guitar at the elbow joint. Those with longer arms will contact the guitar farther along the forearm. Apply only enough weight to hold the guitar. Too much pressure will hinder arm movement. Do not let the edge of the guitar cut into the arm: this can result in severely restricted finger movements. Move the right hand from the first to sixth strings, and back again, by moving the arm from the shoulder. If this movement is hindered, then the head of the guitar should be farther forward, or the bottom rim of the guitar should be turned slightly outward. Do not bring your right shoulder forward.

The following will help refine the position of the guitar:

Height of Guitar: The height of the instrument is determined by the access the left hand has to the full range of the fingerboard. First, play the first fret of the sixth string with the first finger. Then move the hand up the fingerboard so the fourth finger can play the nineteenth fret of the first string. If misalignment of the back and shoulders is needed, then adjustments should be made to raise the guitar. These adjustments can easily be made by changing the position of the upper suction cups or the length of the strap. Do not try to compensate for the guitar being too low by collapsing your lower back or dropping your shoulders. These can put pressure on the nerves and muscles of the lower back and can result in a serious accumulation of tension in the shoulders, which can have a devastating effect on the ability of the fingers, hands, and arms to function well.

---

91) See Appendix Two for information about the Guitar A-Frame Support.
92) Shearer, 12.

Angle of Neck: Finding the most advantageous angle for the neck of the guitar calls for more advanced knowledge of left-hand technique and may not be fully understood until Lesson Four is studied. One important element of left-hand technique is the ability of the forearm to rotate and the elbow to move toward or away from the body to better present the hand to the fingerboard. The angle of the neck of the guitar should permit the left forearm and elbow to maintain a position midway between their two extremes of movement during "normal" playing. The forearm and elbow will then have the maximum freedom of movement in both directions. As will be studied later, these movements can greatly simplify left-hand technique. Experiment with the position of the lower suction cups to change the angle of the neck.

Aguado was clearly aware of the relationship between left-hand efficiency and the height and angle of the neck of the guitar: "The fingers of the left hand lose their stopping strength the more the angle of the neck inclines towards the horizontal, but recover it as the neck is proportionately raised. If the neck is excessively high, it tires the hand."[93]

---

93) Aguado, 177.

Lesson Two

Right-hand Positioning

The aims of right-hand positioning are to position the wrist and right-hand finger joints under the alignment and midrange principles. This will lower tension which will permit higher levels of sensitivity to movement, which will allow finer control and more rapid development of coordination and accuracy.

Procedure

1) **Alignment:** Align the left side of the i knuckle with the side of the wrist and forearm. A straight line connecting the middle and knuckle joints of the m finger will bisect the wrist. The alignment of the wrist with the forearm will result in the fingers striking the string at an oblique angle (the precise angle of attack may actually be determined by the angle of the guitar established in the seating position). Aguado was an advocate of this position. In his method he suggested the following to help find a good position: "(the pupil) should stretch his fingers so as to form a straight line with the forearm, without letting them turn toward the bridge, as tends to happen if the hand is slack..."[94]

2) **Arch:** Arch the wrist slightly to allow the thumb its greatest extension and to position the knuckle and middle joints of the fingers in their midrange position. The relationship between the arch and the position of the fingers is critical; a large arch will cause the fingers to be extended with large angles at their joints. As the arch is decreased, the fingers are drawn into the hand and the angles at their joints decreases. The midrange position of the knuckle and middle joints is determined by the amount of wrist arch. For many guitarists the ideal arch can be realized when the position of the wrist causes the thumb to contact the index finger at the tip joint.

3) **Tilt:** Beginning guitarists may need to tilt the hand slightly inward (pronation) to help the thumb reach the bass strings. This is done by rotating the entire forearm. (This rotation starts at the wrist.) An extreme inward tilt seems to introduce the effects of the quadrige phenomenon. As you gain sensitivity, experiment positioning the wrist in its midrange position between pronation and supination.

---

94) Aquado, 15.

30

Lesson Three

Free Stroke with the Thumb

An effortless thumb stroke is needed for the efficient development of right-hand technique—unneeded tension in the thumb can severely restrict the ability to control the positions and movements of the other fingers. Both Sor and Aguado introduced the thumb stroke before the introduction of right-hand finger alternations.

This is the first opportunity to apply the principles of economical muscular effort and ballistic movement. The combination of these two principles will allow muscular freedom to develop.

Through slow practice, the brain should learn to stimulate only the muscles needed for a given movement. This will eliminate extraneous muscle contractions and tensions. Muscular force should be exerted on a joint only at the beginning of movement. Once a finger begins to move, the inertia of this force causes the finger to complete its movement and follow-through. Extra force should not be applied during movement. While a finger is following-through, muscles controlling the finger joints should release and relax. This technical refinement, perhaps more than any other, contributes to the development of effortless technique.

Aims

1) To extend and flex p mainly at the wrist joint with a slight extension and flexion at the tip joint.

2) To develop muscular freedom by allowing p to follow-through to the side of the i finger after sounding the string (do not stop the thumb in midair, which calls for a tension producing muscle against muscle pull).

3) To move to and from the string as directly as possible and to avoid complex circular movements.

Procedure

1) **Position** the right-hand fingers in their comfortable midrange position and rest the tips of i, m, and a on the first string. This will ensure that the right hand does not move during the thumb stroke.

2) **Preparation:** Extend p from the wrist joint and rest the tip on the third string. Contact the string with a combination of nail and flesh. We will explore this *contact point* in more detail in Lesson Six.

3) **Activation:** Stroke the third string, moving mainly from the wrist joint. The middle joint should be passively fixed. Do not allow the tip joint to bend back—this extreme position will make it difficult to cultivate movements from the wrist joint.

4) **Follow-through:** Let p come to rest against the side of i. Do not try to stop the movement with the opposing muscles. The flexor muscles should release and the thumb should swing freely to the i finger. Proper positioning will make this possible whether i is extended or flexed: do not allow p to pass under the fingers. Fernando Sor makes an important observation about the follow-through: "The thumb should never be directed towards the hollow of the hand, but act with the next finger *[i]* as if going to make a cross with it..."[95]

Andrés Segovia, writing almost 150 years later, echoed Sor's precept: "When the hand is held in the correct playing position the thumb *in action* forms a cross with his brother, the index finger."[96]

95) Sor, 12.
96) Andrés Segovia and George Mendoza, *SEGOVIA: my book of the guitar* (New York: Collins, 1979), 27.

Thumb Stroke Exercises

The following open string exercises should be practiced very slowly at first, with attention paid to the details of positioning and movement. Rest the tips of *i*, *m*, and *a* on the first string and reach back with the thumb from the wrist joint. (If this reach is too much, rest the fingers on the second or third string.) *The hand should not move.* The thumb stroke should be thoroughly mastered before continuing with the study of the left-hand or right-hand finger movements.

Exercise 1:

Exercise 2:

Exercise 3:

Exercise 4:

Exercise 5:

Exercise 6:

Exercise 7:

Exercise 8:

Lesson Four

The Left Hand

The position of the left hand is not static, but dynamic. It is always changing. The left hand must perform countless chord shapes, many of which call for wide reaches and stretches across the width and length of the fingerboard. Movements in and out of these positions call for the hand to move up, down, or across the fingerboard. The advanced literature requires many combinations of these and other activities. This wide range of movement and positioning makes it impractical to suggest one rigid-hand position. Left hand positioning is simply a matter of finding the position that will allow the greatest mechanical advantage to the muscles and joints. This mechanical advantage is defined by the alignment and midrange principles. The following can serve as a guide to dynamic positioning to help discover and maintain a position of greatest mechanical advantage.

Procedure

1) The forearm should remain aligned with the wrist and hand at all times.

2) The left wrist should be slightly arched and the joints of the left-hand fingers should be positioned in their comfortable midrange position, between the extremes of extension and flexion.

3) The left thumb should be positioned behind the neck of the guitar opposite the first finger or second finger. The position of the thumb will vary during guitar playing. The rotation of the left forearm (discussed below) will reposition the thumb between the first and third fingers.

4) The thumb should apply only *minimum pressure* against the back of the neck. When the left hand must cross strings or shift, the thumb should move with the hand while maintaining its position relative to the fingers. The author of *Miss Mary Burwell's Instruction Book for the Lute* wrote in the 1660s: "…the thumb must be as useful and nimble as the fingers."[97] Too much pressure will cause the tip joint to bend back to its limit of extension making any movement difficult and cumbersome. When the thumb grips the neck too hard it cannot be "useful and nimble." Excessive tension in the left-hand thumb is usually a result of excessive force used by the fingers while stopping notes.

5) While forming notes, the joints of the fingers should be as close as possible to their comfortable midrange position. This midrange position can be maintained by observing and manipulating the way the left arm presents the hand to the fingerboard. While the positions providing the greatest mechanical advantage to the muscles and joints of the left hand are diverse and will vary according to context, there are three basic positions:

   a. The knuckle joint of the first finger is closer to the edge of the neck of the fingerboard while the knuckles of two, three, and four are successively farther away.

   b. The knuckle joints of two, three, and four are parallel to the edge of the fingerboard.

   c. The knuckle joint of the fourth finger is closer to the edge of the neck of the guitar while the knuckle joints of three, two, and one are successively farther away.

---

97) Thurston Dart, "Miss Mary Burwell's Instruction Book for the Lute," *Galpin Society Journal,* May 1958, 23.

In simple textures, such as single notes on one string (see Exercises 9-11), a slight rotation of the forearm may be enough to cause these changes. These movements of *pronation* and *supination* begin at the wrist. In more complex textures, movements of the elbow toward or away from the body, coupled with the rotation of the forearm, will further affect the position of the left hand. The movements of the elbow arise from the shoulder. *The left wrist should not deviate from its position of alignment!*

6) The fingers of the left hand should be positioned directly behind their frets, with the *least* amount of pressure needed to obtain clear sounds. The job of the left-hand fingers is not, as many assume, to push the string down to the fingerboard: rather it is to merely hold the string against the fret. As the distance between the finger and the fret increases, the pressure needed of the left-hand fingers also increases. Thus, *the more accurate the fingers are, the less effort they need to form clear notes.* Aguado wrote: "...(place) the fingers of the left hand close behind each fret. It is extremely important to place them here and not elsewhere in the space between frets, because with the slight pressure of the finger, the string necessarily rests on the fret and thus produces a clear sound..."[98]

The studied manipulation of the left arm will help position the tips of the fingers directly behind their frets *without the fingers having to reach.* This will be explored in more detail in Lesson Eighteen. (More experienced students may wish to begin the study of Lesson Eighteen now.)

7) The left-hand fingers will contact the fingerboard at varying angles on varying sides of their tips. The tip segments should not, as is sometimes advocated, try to approach the fingerboard at a perpendicular angle. The fingers are set into the hand at different angles and are not naturally parallel to each other. The effort needed to maintain such a position for the fingers can result in a harmful and serious accumulation of muscular tension.

Aguado originally advocated the tip segments form a perpendicular angle with the fingerboard, but in his Appendix from 1849 he wrote: "The forefinger should play resting the outside of the fleshy part on the strings...the other fingers will have to be placed obliquely to the frets instead of being nearly perpendicular, as I said in paragraphs 68 and 69 of the *New Method.* I can confirm that, according to experiments I have made on myself and my pupils, this form of placing the fingers is very advantageous, and it is not difficult to become used to it."[99]

8) Movement for moving on and off of notes should be made mainly from the knuckle joints. If these joints are not positioned in their midrange position and are close to their limit of extension, extra tension will result when fingers try to move off of their notes. Speed and ease of playing are as much a function of the extensor muscles as they are the flexor muscles. The function of the fourth finger can be greatly enhanced by gaining control of its independent metacarpal.

These movements, as well as the movements of the forearm and elbow, should be the focus of study. Movements should be as smooth as possible. This calls for the ability to anticipate or prepare the movements and positions needed for the next note or group of notes.

9) Unused fingers should remain in their midrange position, close to the fingerboard.

10) The joints of the left-hand fingers should not collapse at any time, except in the case of some intentional advanced technique.

---

98) Aguado, 16.
99) Aguado, 15.

Lesson Five

Left-hand Exercises

The following three exercises are to be played with *p*. They are designed to allow you to study and develop effective left-hand positions while executing simple right-hand thumb movements. Exercises 9 and 10 use open strings and are in the first position. They can also be practiced on the other strings. Exercise 11 can be played on any string in any position.

Observe the following:

1) **Alignment:** The alignment of the left wrist and forearm should be maintained at all times.

2) **Accuracy:** Left-hand fingers should stop notes *directly* behind the frets.

3) If a finger cannot reach behind its fret without overextending from the middle joint, experiment with the rotation of the left forearm. Students having trouble maintaining a midrange position while using the third and fourth fingers may find it helpful to rotate their left forearm so the third and fourth fingers are brought closer to the fingerboard (supination): if the alignment of the left wrist and forearm is maintained, this movement will preserve a position of mechanical advantage. A rotation of the forearm in the opposite direction (pronation) will move the first finger toward the bass side of the neck. These subtle changes of the position of the left hand can be performed either while playing an open string or by pivoting on a stopped note. This pivoting action will be difficult if the fingers are using too much force to stop notes.

Please note, however, that while playing a series of rapid connected notes in one position (such as in scale playing) the hand should not try to change position for each note, although the hand should cross strings as the passage moves across the fingerboard.

4) The left thumb should be positioned between the bass and treble sides of the neck and should exert no noticeable pressure against the back of the neck at this time.

5) Be sensitive to how little pressure the left-hand fingers need to form clear notes. Aguado gives some very specific advice about economical effort: "In the pressure of the fingers on the strings, the strength employed should be no greater than is necessary to produce a clear sound. First place a finger on any fret of any string, at its proper place, but without pressing. When this note is plucked, the sound is blurred because the finger did not press down enough; the pressure should then be experimented with until when the string is plucked the sound is clear and no further pressure is required."[100]

6) Once the left hand is in its best position, the movement for moving on and off of notes should come primarily from the knuckle joints.

7) The position and movement of the right hand and thumb should not be neglected.

---

100) Aguado, 120.

Exercise 9:

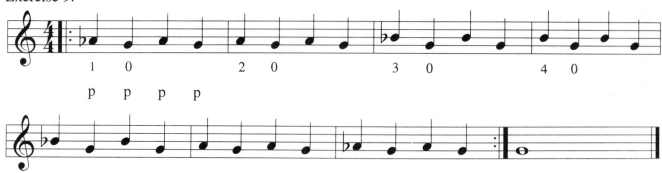

Exercise 10:

Exercise 11:

Lesson Six

Right-hand Finger Strokes[101]

The timing and coordination between alternating right-hand fingers needs to be established for technique to improve beyond the most rudimentary level. What is often overlooked is the timing and coordination between joints of the *same* finger during a finger stroke.

The movements of individual fingers need to be studied and mastered before trying to use these movements in the more demanding contexts of scales and arpeggios. The movement of each finger should be properly trained: this will prevent some of the coordination and tension problems common in the playing of guitarists at all levels.

Before this training can begin, we need to consider the importance of the fingernails and the contact point, the role each finger joint has in the stroke, and the types of flexion and extension.

The Nails and the Contact Point

There is no greater difference among guitarists than that of their fingernails. The nail's composition, shape, and size of the subungle separation (the place where the nail separates from the flesh) are subject to wide variation. Because of these variations, there are no general principles regarding nail shape and length.

The right-hand nails should be kept clean and smooth. Guitarists will normally have to experiment for some time with their nail shape and length. A change in the shape and length of the nails will probably need to accompany a change in hand position or finger stroke, no matter how slight. Don't let a problem with the nail prevent you from experimenting with your technique.

The meeting of string and finger is called the *contact point*. The cultivation of a precise and consistent contact point is one of the goals of right-hand training and is largely responsible for the quality of tone and ease of playing. Guitarists who do not have a secure contact point will often contaminate their strokes with extra effort to clear the string.

Generally, the finger should contact the string with a combination of nail and flesh. This will vary with the length of the nail or the size of the subungle separation. Students with a large separation may find it difficult to contact the string with both nail and flesh and should experiment with the nail only. If the nail is too long it will be difficult to develop a secure contact point. Do not contact the string on the tip segment. It is also important that the finger leave the string at the same contact point—if the finger slides along the string, the nail shape and length, right-hand position, or basic stroke may need to be adjusted. Throughout your development as a guitarist you will continually be refining your contact point.

The Finger Joints

Before refining the positions and movements so that effective rest strokes and free strokes can be performed, it is important to understand the unique contributions each joint makes to the stroke.

The Knuckle Joint: This joint has two functions: 1) Because the knuckle joint is the first joint to release during extension (see page 14), it is largely responsible for releasing the finger back to its midrange position so that the finger can stroke the string again. This joint should be positioned in its midrange position for both rest stroke and free stroke. Beginners and intermediate students may work to extend the finger, but advanced

---

101) Also see Aaron Shearer "Training the Right-hand Fingers" from *Learning the Classic Guitar,* Part One, 49.

guitarists have cultivated the sensitivity to simply release the finger back to its midrange. 2) The knuckle joint is also responsible for controlling the volume of finger strokes. Because this joint is a more distant fulcrum, it has an efficient effect on the speed of the fingertip (see page 15). This quicker movement will transmit more energy to the string and will cause a wider and faster string vibration. More volume requires more force and effort—this extra force must be converted into movement. The knuckle joint should help bring the fingertip to the string and continue its movement through the string into the follow-through. However, do not force the follow-through from this joint.

The Middle Joint: This joint is responsible for the accuracy of free strokes. In free stroke it must be positioned on the flexion side of its midrange to insure that the fingertip can clear the next lower string. If this joint is too extended it will be difficult to clear the lower adjacent string without continuously flexing the tip joint throughout the stroke. In rest stroke the middle joint is positioned on the extension side of its midrange so the fingertip can come to rest on the next lower string. The middle joint does contribute to the stroke and should flex as the finger moves across the string. It should never be kept rigid.

The Tip Joint: This joint should never be kept rigid, and should never actively flex for the duration of a finger stroke. Guitarists needing to reduce the tension in their hands should train the tip joint to gently yield to the resistance of the string in both rest stroke and free stroke. Besides providing greater freedom to the middle and knuckle joints (see pages 12-15), the flexibility of the tip joint will help deflect the string toward the soundboard which will result in a fuller sound. As you progress and your hand becomes more sensitive, experiment with introducing a small amount of tension to the tip joints and releasing it instantly as you stroke.

The Types of Flexion and Extension

Previously learned skills don't remain static or frozen when we improve—new experiences give us fresh insights into concepts we thought we had understood and mastered long ago. This process, recognized or not, is the cause of our most significant technical breakthroughs.

As our sensitivity develops, our finger movements can progress toward greater ease. This concept should encourage students to periodically review or explore the "simple" facets of their technique. There is nothing more "simple" than the different ways of flexing and extending the fingers.

Flexion

There are two ways of flexing the fingers:

1) The flexor muscles can apply force to the joints they control throughout the entire course of movement. These movements are characteristic of beginners and are cumbersome and inefficient. This extra effort is often a result of an inefficient position, of misunderstanding proper movement, or of trying to keep the tip or middle joint rigid. A characteristic problem of this type of flexion is the difficulty in getting the finger back out for its next stroke. It is not necessarily wrong for beginners to play this way, but as they acquire more sensitivity, refining their strokes should be a priority.

2) The flexor muscles contract and then immediately relax. The finger then can complete its movement effortlessly and easily release back to its midrange position. These movements are fluid and graceful and are characteristic of more advanced playing. (See the principles of economical effort and ballistic movement on page 23.) Remember that loud playing should not be the result of extra force that is not turned into movement. Volume is a result of the strength of the muscular contraction at the knuckle joint. This will cause the fingertip to move through the string more quickly. The muscles still relax immediately after their contraction.

38

Extension

The extension of the fingers is often neglected by teachers and method books. But it is the ability of a finger to be ready for its next movement that contributes to speed. The way a finger extends or releases can either contribute to or interfere with this readiness. There are three ways of extending the fingers:

1) Continuous effort is applied by the extensor muscles to the finger joints throughout the duration of the movement. As in the first type of flexion, this type of extension is usually the only way beginners can control their fingers but it is cumbersome and requires too much effort. This extra effort may also be the result of improper positioning or movement.

2) The next type of extension corresponds to the second type of flexion. The extensor muscles contract and then instantly relax. This contraction sends the finger out past its string. This type of extension is used by intermediate (and some advanced) guitarists. It is effective but requires much sensitivity to the small amount of force required for the extension. There is a danger of overextension.

   There is also a related type of extension: the extensor muscles contract sending the finger out past its string, then the flexor muscles contract to stop the movement in an errant attempt to conform to the so-called principle of "economy of movement." This produces a potentially damaging and tiring muscle against muscle pull. True economy of movement is a result of economy of effort.

3) There is a third type of extension which is very difficult to describe and even harder to know how to practice. It is the *release*. The sensation is of a finger releasing itself back to its midrange position without the active participation of the extensor muscles. This is why the wrist and fingers must be positioned so that the midrange position allows the fingertips to fall just outside their strings. This type of movement is used by very advanced players, even though they might not be aware of it.

One guitarist who is aware of the release is Pepe Romero. He writes: "…the initial impulse that causes the finger to release[102] the string and set it in vibration is the same impulse that brings the finger back again to playing position, without ever reversing the natural movement of the finger."[103] His description is a little confusing because certainly the movement of the finger is reversed, but the image of the sensation is a useful one.

It would take sophisticated electromyographic studies to determine if the extensor muscles were actually silent during this type of movement. It is possible that the release is actually the manifestation of the minimum effort needed to bring the finger back to its string.

The study of these movements on open strings and the practice of simple exercises is some of the major work advanced guitar students can do. These procedures and simple exercises should be studied slowly and carefully. The following, presented for the *i* finger, should be repeated for each finger.

Rest Stroke and Free Stroke

The free stroke (tirando) and the rest stroke (apoyando) are usually defined by the path of the finger after it strokes its string: the finger passes freely above the next lower string in free stroke and comes to rest against the next lower string in rest stroke. This difference in the path of the fingertip requires a different angle at the middle joint for the two strokes. While playing a rest stroke on the first string, the middle joint is positioned toward the extension side of its midrange position; while playing a free stroke on the third string, the middle joint is positioned toward the flexion side of its midrange position. This difference is vital to allow the finger to complete its stroke comfortably and accurately. The angle at the knuckle joint may vary only slightly. The

---

102) Do not confuse Romero's idea of the finger releasing the string (stroking) with the concept of the muscles releasing the finger back to its midrange.
103) Romero, 10.

cultivation of the most advantageous position of the fingers will make it possible for *a* to extend comfortably without approaching its limit of extension and introducing the negative effects of the quadrige phenomenon on the *m* finger.

Free Stroke: Positioning and Movement

1) **Position** the wrist in its midrange position. This will place the knuckle and middle joints in their comfortable midrange position. Move the hand to the guitar so the fingertip of *i* falls just outside the third string. If learning to let your tip joints give during the stroke you will need to position your middle joint slightly more toward the flexion side of midrange.

2) **Prepare** the tip of *i* on the third string. This preparation will give you time to refine your contact point. The preparation also helps establish the precise timing between the middle joint and the knuckle joint (see Lesson Eight).

3) **Stroke** the string while pulling through from the knuckle and middle joints. The middle joint must be positioned to allow the finger to follow-through above the fourth string. Do not force the follow-through: simply allow the finger to move freely from the first muscular impulse. If you are studying to discover the minimal effort you need to perform a stroke, the tip joint should give as it moves through the string. More advanced students should experiment with a little firmness at the tip joints and then release it instantly. In any case, the tip joint should not be under continuous tension.

Let the muscles release and relax as the finger makes its movement through the string. Muscular effort should not be applied during the finger movement.

4) **Release**. Release the finger back to its midrange position. Beginners may need to make a coordinated extension from the knuckle and middle joints so the fingertip will be just beyond the third string. The finger should not straighten.

5) **Flex** *i* slightly to return to the string to prepare for the next stroke. Feel the coordinated movement of the knuckle and middle joints as they return to the string.

6) **Repeat**. Practice separately with *m* and *a*. The *a* finger and the little finger should move when *m* strokes; the little finger should move when *a* strokes.

Exercise 12: Free Stroke

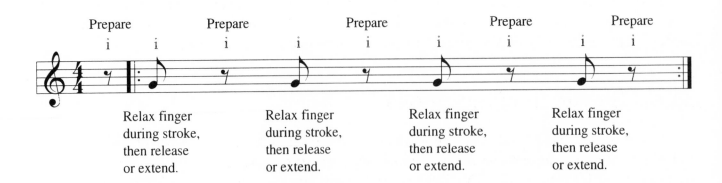

Rest Stroke: Positioning and Movement

1) **Position** the knuckle joints so they are in their midrange position. Position the middle joints closer to the extension side of their midrange position.

2) **Prepare** the tip of i on the first string. The contact point is of equal importance in rest stroke. The preparation will also help establish the precise timing of the middle joint with the knuckle joint.

3) **Stroke** the string while pulling through from the middle joint to bring the finger to rest against the second string. The tip joint should not be under continuous tension. While movement from the knuckle joint helped to bring the finger to the string, the stroke must come from the middle joint.

Let the muscles release and relax as the finger makes its movement through the string. Muscular effort should not be applied during the finger movement.

4) **Release.** Release the finger back to its midrange position. Beginners may need to make a coordinated extension from the knuckle and middle joints so the fingertip will be just beyond the first string. The finger should not straighten.

5) **Flex** i and return to the string to prepare for the next stroke. Feel the coordinated movement of the knuckle and middle joints as they return to the string.

6) **Repeat.** Practice separately with m and a. The a finger and the little finger should move when m strokes; the little finger should move when a strokes

Exercise 13: Rest Stroke

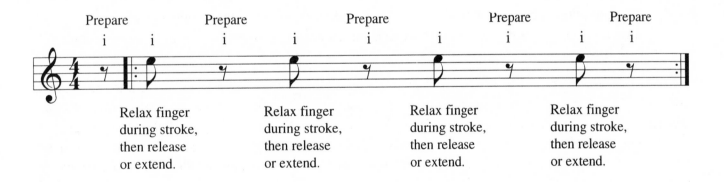

41

Lesson Seven
Right-hand Finger Alternations

The most common use of right-hand fingers is the continuous alternation between two fingers. Simply stated, one finger flexes as the other extends or releases. There is a change of direction at the end of both flexion and extension, although at rapid tempos movements are fluid and continuous. During early slow practice the extension and flexion should aim to establish timing, coordination, and muscular freedom. Circular or oval movements, which call for the simultaneous extension at the knuckle joint and flexion at the middle joint, should be avoided.

Alternation should not be tried until the movements of individual fingers have been developed.

The successful mastery of finger alternations also means developing the control of fingers not directly used in the alternation.[104] Tension present in the unused fingers can adversely affect the freedom of movement of the other fingers. While studying the alternations for the three pairs of fingers, the following will help develop muscular freedom:

1) When alternating i and m, a and c (the little finger) should move with m. Be sure to keep the tip joints of a and c free of tension.

2) When alternating m and a, c should move with a; i remains at its midrange. The tip joint of a should be free of tension. Avoid exaggerating the flexion of m and extension of a—this will introduce the adverse effects of the quadrige phenomenon.

3) When alternating i and a, c should move with a; m should remain at its midrange position. Do not hold m stiffly in position—it can move when a moves. Again, all tension in the tip joint of c should be eliminated.

Cultivate sensitivity to the minimum amount of muscular effort needed. Muscular contractions should arise quickly and immediately be replaced with relaxations. The difficulty in advanced alternations is timing the release of one finger with the stroke of the other. Although this can be practiced at a slow tempo, the movements themselves cannot be practiced slowly—they would no longer be ballistic. Therefore right-hand finger alternations will need to be studied on two levels. The first level will help develop the precise exchange between fingers. Most beginners and some intermediate students will need to practice this way. The second level will help develop the release.

The following steps should be applied to free stroke on the third string and rest stroke on the first string.

To Develop A Precise Exchange

1) **Prepare:** Position the tip of i on the string. Find your contact point. Eventually this preparation will be eliminated and the fingers will "prepare" just outside their strings.

2) **Alternate:** At the instant i flexes and strokes its string, extend m out beyond the string. Be sure to let i follow-through back toward the palm. Do not exaggerate this follow-through: it should be the result of the muscular contraction at the start of the stroke.

3) **Prepare:** Bring m to the string. The i finger should still be in its follow-through position.

---

104) See Shearer, 49, 50.

42

4) **Alternate:** Flex *m* and follow-through. At the instant *m* flexes, extend *i*.

5) **Repeat**. The same steps should be studied with *m-a* and *i-a*.

Exercise 14: Free Stroke:

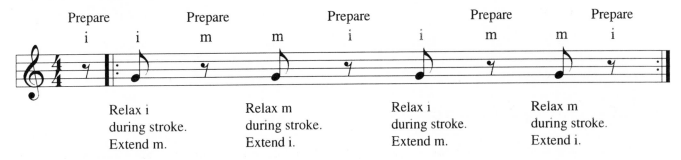

Relax i during stroke. Extend m.

Relax m during stroke. Extend i.

Relax i during stroke. Extend m.

Relax m during stroke. Extend i.

Exercise 15: Rest Stroke:

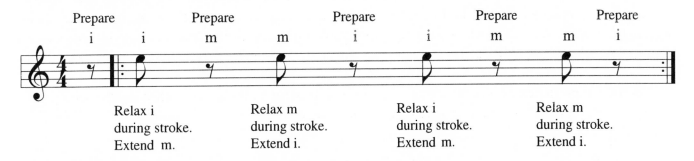

Relax i during stroke. Extend m.

Relax m during stroke. Extend i.

Relax i during stroke. Extend m.

Relax m during stroke. Extend i.

To Develop The Release

1) **Prepare:** Position the tip of *i* on the string. Find your contact point. Eventually this preparation will be eliminated and the fingers will "prepare" just outside their strings.

2) **Stroke and Release** with *i*. After *i* flexes and sounds its string, allow it to freely release back to its midrange position.

3) **Prepare:** Bring *m* to the string and prepare. The *i* finger should still be positioned in its midrange position just outside the string.

4) **Stroke and Release** with *m*. After *m* flexes and sounds its string, allow it to freely release back to its midrange.

5) **Repeat**. The same steps should be studied with *m-a* and *i-a*.

Exercise 16: Free Stroke:

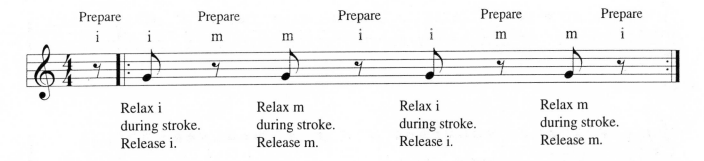

Relax i during stroke. Release i.

Relax m during stroke. Release m.

Relax i during stroke. Release i.

Relax m during stroke. Release m.

Exercise 17: Rest Stroke:

Open String Exercises

Effective right-hand finger alternations can only be properly developed through open-string work. Trying to use the left hand will introduce coordination and timing problems for which the hands and mind are not yet prepared. The simple repetition of these movements is the surest and quickest way to establish these strokes. The following exercises for free stroke on the third string and rest stroke on the first string should be practiced daily, with and without the preparation. Study them carefully, and attend to the position and movement of the fingers. Although the exercises are fingered for *i-m* and *m-i*, they should also be studied with *m-a, a-m, i-a,* and *a-i.*

As the tempo increases, the release of one finger will occur as the other is stroking the string. This effortless feeling is an essential component of advanced technique.

Free Stroke Exercises

Exercise 18:

Exercise 19:

Rest Stroke Exercises

Exercise 20:

Exercise 21:

Lesson Eight

The Prepared Stroke

The use of the prepared stroke in guitar training has caused substantial misunderstanding and divisiveness among guitarists and teachers. When properly understood and applied in early training, the prepared stroke can hasten the development of several important skills. It should not be the foundation of any pedagogical approach, but is simply a helpful practice technique.

Although a preparation was used in Lessons Six and Seven, a more detailed explanation will encourage advanced study.

Preparing the tip of the finger on the string before the string is to be sounded does several things:

1) Coordination and Timing

The prepared stroke helps develop the coordination and exact timing between the knuckle and middle joints: the point of preparation is the point where the middle joint contributes to the stroke.

2) Clear and Concise Alternation

The preparation contributes to a clear and concise alternation by defining the precise moment of exchange between alternating fingers.

3) Development of Tone

The prepared stroke allows time to develop a more precise and consistent placement of the nail and flesh on the string. The consistency and security of this contact point is essential for advanced playing.

4) Development of Velocity

By playing a shorter or longer staccato (a result of the preparation), the speed of individual finger movements can be varied *without increasing the tempo*. This allows you to simulate and control certain aspects of high velocity playing before high velocity can be reached, which will hasten its development. Speed is as much a function of the ability to release a finger back to its midrange as it is a function of the efficient use of the flexor muscles. The preparation can help train the efficient release of the fingers.

The preparation should come during the flexion part of the stroke, and not at the end of the extension or release—it is important the fingers be trained to perform a coordinated release slightly *beyond* the string (this will be the midrange position) before they return to the string to prepare. It is the size of this movement out beyond the string and the way the finger changes direction that account for the easy velocity attained by highly proficient guitarists.

The practice of the prepared stroke in finger alternations can help aspiring virtuosi study a crucial problem: how to make smaller finger movements while still providing muscular freedom to their muscles. This freedom is a result of economical efforts and ballistic movements. (The prepared stroke can also help the development of arpeggio technique—this will be discussed in Lesson Fourteen.) These smaller movements are vital for the great speed required by the advanced literature. The ease and endurance needed to maintain this speed are a product of muscular freedom. These smaller movements should be the result of a finely calculated release of the finger back to its midrange position — they should not result from the muscle against muscle pull of the flexor muscle acting as a "brake" for the extensor muscle. This muscle against muscle pull will cause added tension.

45

In the following two exercises, the staccato quarter notes allow time to prepare the fingers and study these refined movements; the eighth notes will allow the opportunity to incorporate these refinements into an unprepared stroke.

Exercise 22: (rest stroke)

Exercise 23: (free stroke)

Lesson Nine

Coordination Exercises

The following three exercises will help develop the timing and coordination between the two hands. You should become increasingly sensitive to the tension in each hand. The successful consolidation of the techniques for both hands is the foremost goal of early training. Failure to understand the significance of this goal can lead to the development of many problems: tension in one part of the body can be transferred through the central nervous system to other parts of the body. This is especially common between the left and right hands in guitar playing. A problem in one hand will often manifest itself in the other hand. The inability to define the specific causes of problems can make the study of advanced technique very difficult and frustrating.

Although the exercises are fingered for *i-m* and *m-i,* they should also be practiced with *m-a, a-m, i-a,* and *a-i,* rest stroke and free stroke.

Ascend position with each repetition.

Exercise 24:

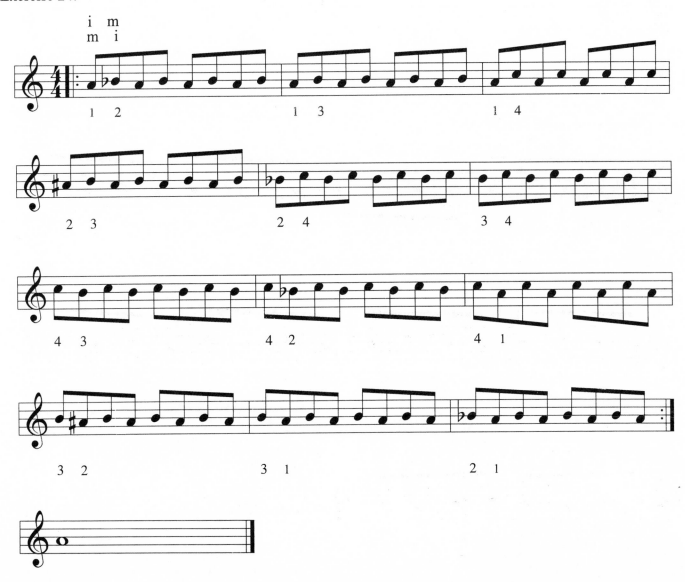

47

Exercise 25:

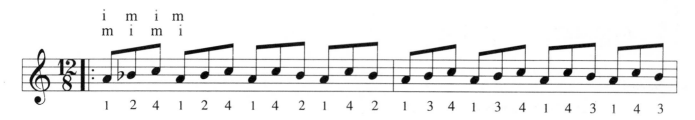

Exercise 26:

Lesson Ten

String Crossing

The lack of a focused study of string crossing may be the major cause of many students' inability to perform rapid scales convincingly. Students are so preoccupied with the more obvious aspects of scale technique (shifting and right-hand speed), they don't realize the importance of controlling the movement of the right hand from string to string to preserve the most effective right-hand and finger positions. The following exercises are designed so students at all levels can develop or refine their string-crossing technique.

Refined string-crossing technique requires the entire arm to be moved up or down across the strings from the shoulder. This will allow the hand to be repositioned to play on any string while preserving the most beneficial finger/string relationship. Short crosses of one or two strings may be performed by moving the forearm up and down from the elbow.

Students should begin the study of Exercises 27 and 28 by moving the arm, from the shoulder, precisely the distance to the next string. The rests in these exercises will allow time to perform the cross and to check that the proper wrist and finger joint relationships are maintained. The remaining exercises gradually increase in difficulty. It will be helpful to perform the cross while the last finger to play a string is following-through.

Although you may feel more comfortable practicing these exercises free stroke, rest stroke string crossing is more difficult and should be the object of advanced study. All string crossing exercises should be studied with *m-a, a-m, i-a, a-i,* aside from *i-m* and *m-i.*

Exercise 27:

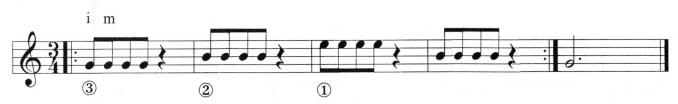

Exercise 28:

Exercise 29:

49

Exercise 30:

Exercise 31:

Exercise 32:

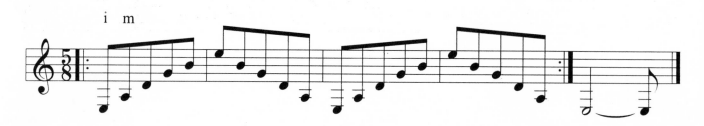

Advanced students may benefit from practicing the following exercises on *Guardame Las Vacas* and *Folias de España,* two popular chord progressions and the bases of many variations for solo guitar. They should be studied with rest stroke and free stroke. Exercises fingered for *m-i* should also be studied with *a-m* and *a-i*. Exercises fingered for *i-m* should be studied with *m-a* and *i-a*.

String Crossing Variations on Las Vacas

Exercise 33:

Exercise 34:

51

String Crossing Variations on Folias

Exercise 35:

Exercise 36:

Lesson Eleven

Consolidation Exercises

The following important exercises will help consolidate the different techniques for the left and right hands and will serve as preparation for scale playing. Pay special attention to the string crossing of *both* hands. Each exercise should be played rest stroke and free stroke, *i-m, m-a,* and *i-a.*

Exercises not using open strings can be practiced in successively higher positions with each repetition.

Exercise 37:

Exercise 38:

53

Exercise 39:

Exercise 40:

Exercise 41:

Exercise 42:

Exercise 43:

Exercise 44:

Exercise 45:

Exercise 46:

Lesson Twelve

Fingers Together

When two or three right-hand fingers play notes together, they should be in their free-stroke position and follow-through as they normally would after sounding their strings. Strive to sound the notes at precisely the same time.

Exercise 47:

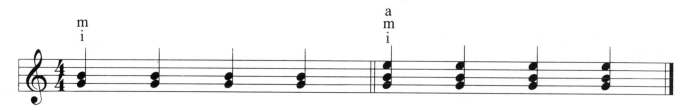

Exercise 48: (Lesson Six from Aguado's *New Guitar Method*)

Lesson Thirteen

Thumb and Fingers Together

Most of the music played on the guitar, from two-voice textures to block chords and arpeggios, requires the thumb and fingers to work together. This coordination between the two, although not difficult to establish, does need to be studied and practiced.

When the thumb plays with the fingers, it follows-through as it normally would and should come to rest against the side of the i finger. The fingers follow-through toward the palm of the hand. One of Aguado's first lessons dealt with this movement: "When the right thumb and forefinger pluck two strings at the same time, the action of the forefinger should be towards the palm of the hand, while the thumb...should be above the forefinger after plucking, making a kind of cross."[105]

Exercise 49:

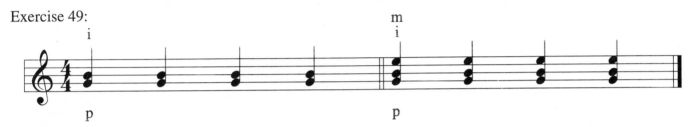

The following exercise is from Mauro Giuliani's *Studio per la chitarra,* Op. 1, published in Vienna in 1812.

Exercise 50:

When the thumb and a finger alternate, the movements are a little more detailed. In this exercise from Aguado's seventh lesson, the i finger should extend or release at the instant p makes its stroke. This needs to be studied carefully: although the i finger has returned to its midrange, the thumb should still be able to follow-through against it. At the instant the i finger strokes, p should extend. If the i finger is not used and the alternation is between p and m or p and a, it should remain in its midrange position for the thumb follow-through. The development of this "reciprocal" movement is vital to the successful execution of a variety of musical textures.

This exercise should also be practiced with p-m.

105) Aguado, 15.

Exercise 51: (Lesson Seven from Aguado's *New Guitar Method*)

Lesson Fourteen
Arpeggio Movements

Although there are myriad arpeggio patterns, there are really only two types of patterns: those using sympathetic motion of the fingers, and those using opposed motion of the fingers. Sympathetic motion requires that the fingers move in "sympathy," that is, fingers flex together or in sequence—no finger extends during this flexion. In a sympathetic movement of the fingers, each finger can be used only once between thumb strokes. The flexion and extension or release of the fingers is felt as one unified movement. This movement is nothing more than a reciprocal alternation between the thumb and fingers.

The introduction of opposed motion, while creating more possibilities, does create potential technical problems. The exchange between fingers needs to be clearly defined and studied.

The following should be observed during the first practice of all patterns:

1) Start at a slow tempo, and repeat patterns evenly. This is to discover the timing and coordination needed to take advantage of the "reflexive" nature of sympathetic motion, and to define the precise exchange between fingers in those patterns using opposed motion.

2) The thumb should play a bass string and alternate with the last finger in a pattern.

3) The little finger (c) should remain free of tension and move with a at all times. If a is not used in a pattern, it should move with m.

4) After stroking its string, the thumb should be able to come to rest against the side of i after its follow-through. This should be possible whether the i finger is extended or flexed. If the thumb passes under the fingers, the arch of the wrist may need to be adjusted to change the angle at the knuckle joints, or the extension of i should be reduced slightly. The thumb stroke is an important part of arpeggio technique—unneeded tension in the thumb can quickly inhibit the ability to control the fingers.

5) The flexion of a finger calls for a follow-through from the middle joint. While some follow-through from the knuckle joint should be present, do not exaggerate this movement.

6) Once the patterns are memorized and habitual, practice exercises 52, 53, and 54.

7) After the patterns become organized and comfortable at higher speeds, restudy them and apply the concept of release: during slow practice each finger can release right after its stroke. As the speed increases, the release will become integrated into a fluid movement. The fingers (especially $i)$ will be able to move back to their midrange position well before their next stroke.

Group One Patterns

Patterns with *p:* sympathetic motion between fingers

1) p-i-m

p flexes... i flexes ....m flexes

(i-m extend) ....p extends)

2) p-m-a

p flexes.. m flexes .... a flexes

(m-a extend) .... (p extends)

3) p-m-i

p flexes.. m flexes ....i flexes

(i-m extend) .... (p extends)

4) p-a-m

p flexes.. a flexes ....m flexes

(m-a extend) .... (p extends)

5) p-i-a

p flexes.. i flexes .... a flexes

(i-a extend) .... (p extends)

6) p-a-i

p flexes.. a flexes ....i flexes

(i-a extend) .... (p extends)

7) p-i-m-a

p flexes.............................. i flexes .... m flexes .... a flexes

(i-m-a extend) .... (p extends)

Exercise 52:

Group Two Patterns

Patterns without *p:* opposed motion between fingers[106]

1) i-m-a

i flexes .... m flexes .... a flexes

(m-a extend) .... (i extends)

2) a-m-i

a flexes .... m flexes .... i flexes

(i extends) .... (m-a extend)

3) i-m-a-m[107]

i flexes .... m flexes .... a flexes .... m flexes

(m-a extend) .... (i-m extend)

4) i-a-m-a

i flexes .... a flexes .... m flexes .... a flexes

(m-a extend) .... (a extends) .... (i extends)

5) a-i-m-i

a flexes .... i flexes .... m flexes .... i flexes

(i extends) .... (a extends) .... (i extends) .... (m-a extend)

(a flexes with m)

Exercise 53:

106) These patterns can also be practiced on single strings by more advanced students. Some of the patterns may work well for rapid scales once the movements have been mastered.
See Lessons Twenty-Two and Twenty-Three.
107) This pattern more commonly appears as a-m-i-m, for example: Carcassi's *Op. 60,* no. 19.

Group Three Patterns

Patterns with *p*: opposed motion between fingers

1) p-i-m-i

p flexes .... i flexes .... m flexes .... i flexes

(i-m extend) .... (i extends) .... (p extends)

2) p-m-a-m

p flexes .... m flexes .... a flexes .... m flexes

(m-a extend) .... (m extends) .... (p extends)

3) p-m-i-m

p flexes .... m flexes .... i flexes .... m flexes

(i-m extend) .... (m extends) .... (p extends)

4) p-a-m-a

p flexes .... a flexes .... m flexes .... a flexes

(m-a extend) .... (a extends) .... (p extends)

5) p-i-a-i

p flexes .... i flexes .... a flexes .... i flexes

(i-a extend) .... (i extends) .... (p extends)

6) p-a-i-a

p flexes .... a flexes .... i flexes .... a flexes

(i-a extend) .... (i extends) .... (p extends)

7) p-i-m-a-m-i

p flexes .... i flexes .... m flexes .... a flexes .... m flexes .... i flexes

(i-m-a extend) .... (i-m extend) .... (p extends)

8) p-m-i-a-m-a[108]

p flexes .... m flexes .... i flexes .... a flexes .... m flexes .... a flexes

(i-m-a extend)(a flexes .... (m-a extend) .... (a extends) ... (p extends)
           with m)

108) This is the movement used in Heitor Villa-Lobos' *Etude No. 1.*

Exercise 54:

The p-a-m-i Arpeggio

Although the *p-a-m-i* arpeggio movement, widely used for tremolo, may seem to fall in the category of sympathetic motion, it is better studied as a pattern requiring opposed motion between *i* and *m*. The *a* finger is the slowest of the three commonly used fingers[109] and will have difficulty extending and then immediately flexing as the first finger to play after the thumb. A better solution is to place an alternation between *i* and *m-a*. This will give the *a* finger ample time to comfortably extend. At high speeds the fingers will be sensed as releasing immediately after their strokes.

p-a-m-i

p flexes .... a flexes .... m flexes ....i flexes

(i extends) .... (p-m-a extend)

Exercise 55:

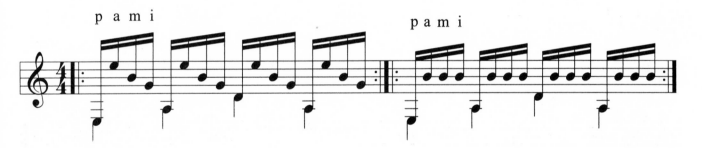

109) See page 18.

The Prepared Arpeggio

Once the arpeggio patterns have been learned, it will be beneficial to study their movements with a "full preparation." This full preparation should not affect the development of sympathetic or opposed motion: after extending a finger or group of fingers, they should immediately return to their strings to prepare. As studied in Lesson Eight, this preparation should come during the flexion part of the stroke, not at the culmination of extension. This is a practice technique to develop smaller and more precise finger movements while providing muscular freedom to the muscles. During actual playing, the fingers "prepare" just outside the string.

The following examples will show the application of this technique in the contexts of sympathetic and opposed motion:

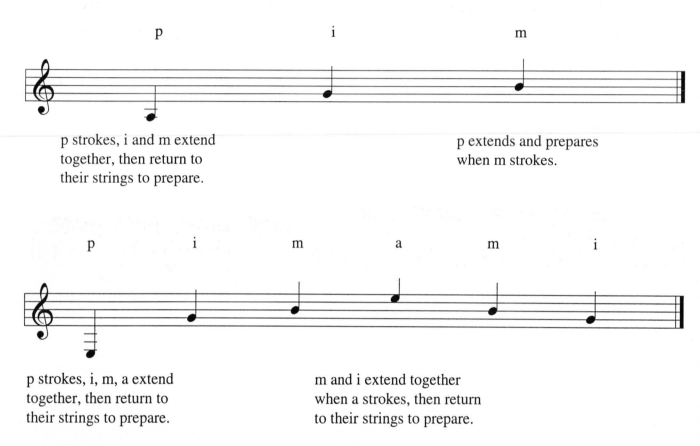

p strokes, i and m extend
together, then return to
their strings to prepare.

p extends and prepares
when m strokes.

p strokes, i, m, a extend
together, then return to
their strings to prepare.

m and i extend together
when a strokes, then return
to their strings to prepare.

A related useful practice technique is the "sequential preparation." Here each finger will prepare as the preceding finger is making its stroke.

66

 esson Fifteen

Giuliani Revisited[110]

Although Nineteenth-Century guitar methods by Fernando Sor, Matteo Carcassi, and Ferdinando Carulli all had arpeggio exercises similar to these, it was the first part of Mauro Giuliani's *Studio per la chitarra,* Op. 1, that served as a model for the following exercises.

Once the movements from Lesson Fourteen have been thoroughly refined and mastered, the daily practice of the following exercises should begin. First practice these exercises at a slow tempo with the full or sequential preparation. Finally, each exercise should be practiced for speed without the preparation. Gradually increase the tempo with each repetition. The rhythmic variants will allow you to focus on a specific part of the arpeggio pattern.

The rhythmic variants can also serve as formulae to be applied as a practice technique to other exercises or portions of pieces.

Exercise 56:

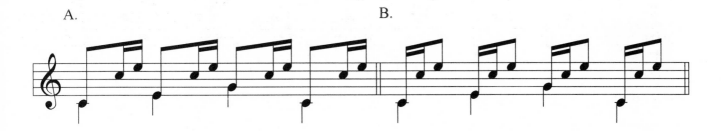

---

110) See my *Giuliani Revisited* (Pacific, MO: Mel Bay Publications, Inc., 1997) for a more extensive treatment of arpeggio practice.

Exercise 57:

A.   B.

Exercise 58:

A.   B.

Exercise 59

A.   B.

Exercise 60:

A.

B.

C.

Exercise 61:

A.

B.

Exercise 62:

A.

B.

Exercise 63:

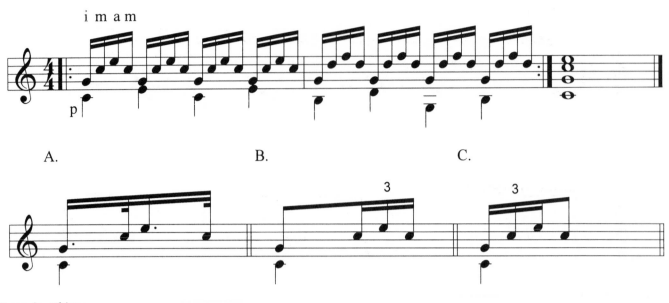

A.   B.   C.

Exercise 64:

A.   B.   C.

Exercise 65:

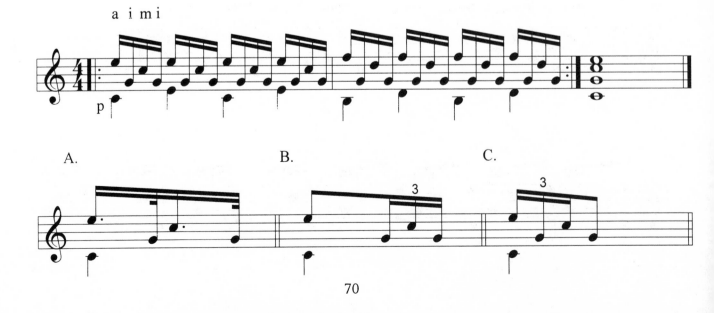

A.   B.   C.

70

Exercise 66:

Exercise 67:

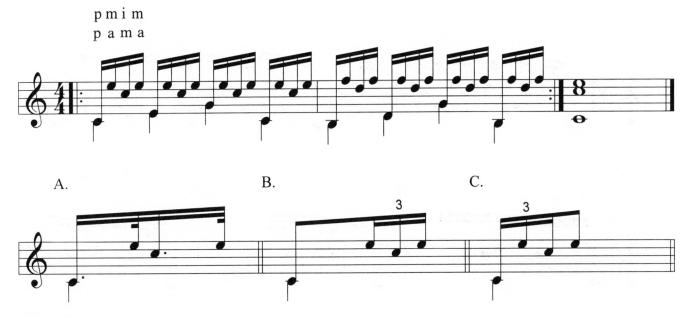

Exercise 68:

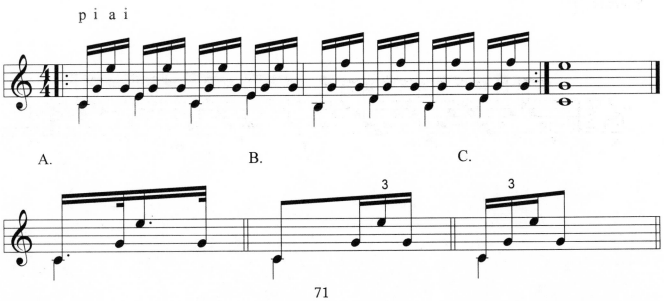

Exercise 69:

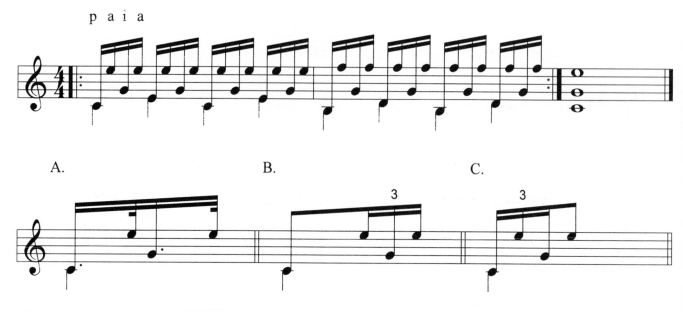

Exercise 70:

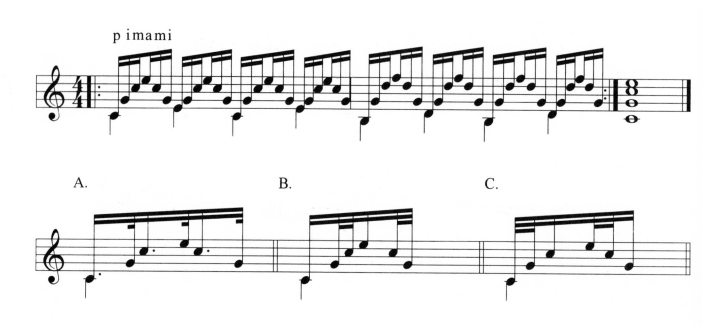

Exercise 71:

Exercise 72:

A. B. C.

Exercise 73:

A. B. C.

Exercise 74:

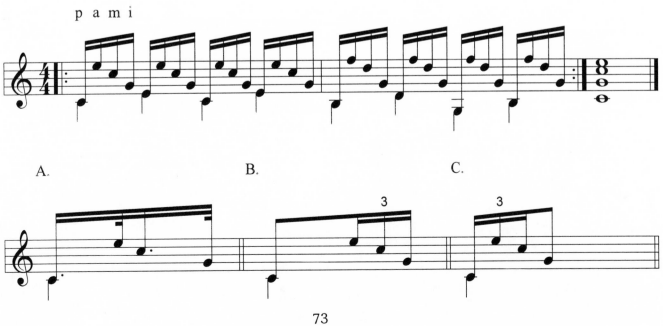

A. B. C.

73

Exercise 75:

A. B. C.

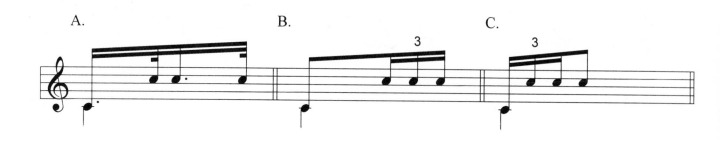

Lesson Sixteen

Speed and Coordination Drills

The first of the following three exercises will help intermediate and advanced students methodically develop the speed of right-hand finger alternations. The next two exercises can help develop that speed in more demanding contexts. Each exercise should be practiced daily with a metronome, rest stroke and free stroke. Increase the speed with each repetition. Although the exercises are fingered for m-i, they should also be studied with a-m and a-i.

In Exercise 76 pay special attention to the coordination between adjacent fingers and adjacent joints of the same finger. Try for an effortless quality to all movements, whatever the tempo, and for an increased sensitivity to tension. Study the prepared stroke while playing the staccato notes (see Lesson Eight), and focus on the effortless release and flexion of individual fingers while playing the dotted rhythms. This exercise should be played twice at each metronome setting: this will allow i-m to be used for the repetition.

Exercise 76:

Exercise 77: (repeat each measure)

75

Exercise 78:

Ascend position after each repetition. When the ninth position is reached, descend.

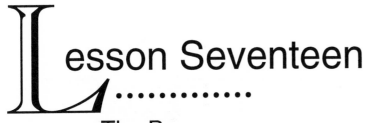

Lesson Seventeen

The Bar

One area of technique presenting obvious difficulties to beginning and intermediate students is the use of the first finger in what are commonly termed "bar chords." Many guitarists labor under the notion that the bar requires an extremely strong left hand. Although some situations calling for use of the bar demand strength and endurance, there are many other instances where an understanding of proper positioning can lead to quick mastery.

Some problems can be solved by understanding exactly how many strings the first finger should cover. Because the first finger can bar across between two and six strings, there is a need for fingering notation to reflect this with precision: an uppercase letter B shows that a bar is needed, a Roman numeral (such as II) will tell the fret, and an Arabic number within a circle, placed to the right and slightly above the Roman numeral, will reveal the number of strings required for the bar.[111] In many cases the first finger will bar across more strings than actually needed so that it is better prepared for the next note or chord.

There are also many situations where the first finger only needs to stop the notes on the outer strings. In the example below, the bar is needed to stop notes on first and fifth strings—the notes in between are stopped by the other fingers:

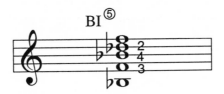

The base of the first finger stops the f on the first string while the tip of the first finger stops the b flat on the fifth string. The first finger should not be exerting force on the second, third, and fourth strings. This can best be done by curving the first finger at the middle joint. The curve will depend on the length of the finger. Some experimentation will be needed to find the best position for the base of the finger to effectively stop notes on the first string.

The following chord presents more of a problem because the first finger must stop notes on the first, third, and sixth strings:

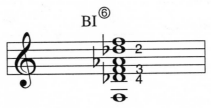

The first finger will need to be straighter than in the previous example and will have to apply force to all the strings. Bars of this type are less common.

The following exercises, modeled after some of Francisco Tarrega's, offer excellent practice for the bar and string crossing. They should be studied with the right-hand patterns on the next page. Advanced students may also practice these chords with different arpeggio patterns.

---

111) Many older editions of guitar music use the symbols 1/2 B or 1/2 C for a bar covering two to five strings. The Guitar Foundation of America is working on a notation manual to encourage editors to be more specific.

Exercise 79:

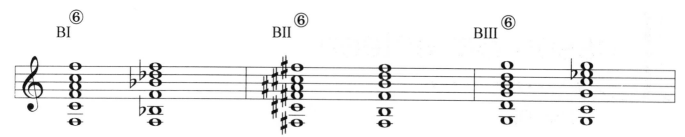

Continue ascending to the eighth position, then return to the first position.

Exercise 80:

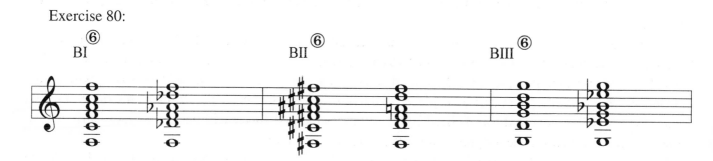

The preceding exercises should be practiced with the following string-crossing patterns. Many endurance problems can be solved in textures similar to these by "rolling" the left hand pressure across the neck of the guitar as the right hand ascends and descends. It is often not necessary to apply pressure to all the notes at once.

Lesson Eighteen

Left-Hand Finger Independence

While the subtle manipulation of the left forearm and elbow to better present the hand and fingers to the fingerboard was discussed earlier, the real rewards of this technical refinement will be apparent in more complex musical textures. The problems of finger independence (the ability to hold down some fingers while moving others) can be lessened and problems of reach can often be solved easily. The closer the left wrist and finger joints can adhere to a mechanically advantageous position, the easier it will be to play the guitar. In some instances, a pronounced movement of the left elbow toward or from the body, combined with the rotation of the forearm, will help the fingers find the position closest to their midrange. These movements, if properly studied, will naturally bring the tips of the fingers closer to their frets, making excessive force or reaching with the fingers unnecessary. These adjustments will let you be more accurate and hold many difficult positions with great ease.

The relative positions of the first and fourth fingers provide useful criteria for studying the rotation of the forearm and the movement of the left elbow. In the example below, supination of the forearm will help move the fourth finger toward the sixth string. The first finger is automatically positioned closer to the treble side of the neck. Positioning is further improved as the left elbow moves in toward the body. It may not always be possible to maintain a midrange position for the joints of both fingers at all times. The resulting position will allow the reach to be taken with the index finger, which has greater independence in extension and can easily move from side to side,[112] while the fourth finger can maintain its midrange position. Intelligent experimenting can help you discover the least difficult way to execute a given chord shape. The position of the left thumb has now moved opposite the third finger.

Conversely, in the next example, pronation of the forearm can help bring the first finger to a more advantageous position for playing on the sixth string. The fourth finger is automatically moved toward the first string. Again, positioning is further improved as the movement of the elbow becomes more pronounced, this time away from the body. The left thumb is now opposite the first finger.

---

112) See page 16.

79

Although Fernando Sor's thoughts on this element of technique have been presented, in his method he presents an arrangement of a portion of the first part of Haydn's oratorio, *The Creation,* for voice and guitar. Using an excerpt from this, he offers a valuable example of how he applies these concepts:

In the second half of the first measure, I am obliged to bring (the elbow) near the body, that the little finger may be found naturally near the sixth string, to press it at the fourth fret. In this case, the second finger is the pivot on which the hand turns. For the commencement of the following measure, I not only direct the elbow to its usual position, but raise it higher, that the tips of my second, third, and fourth fingers, may be found naturally in a line parallel to the frets.[113]

Lesson Nineteen

Independence Exercises

The following left-hand exercises are designed to aid the development of finger independence and reach. Practice should be slow. Study the relationships between the positions and movements of the forearm and elbow, and the resulting positions of the left hand and fingers. The studied manipulation of the arm can make it possible to discover the most efficient position for any chord. Once the most effective positions are found, the movements in and out of those positions should be the focus of study—train the fingers to move slowly and smoothly to their notes (avoid sudden or jerky movements); prepare or anticipate notes. The ability to direct attention to the means of moving from note to note will contribute to smooth, legato playing.

Remember to position the fingers directly behind the fret. This accuracy will allow you to form notes with the least amount of pressure.

The following aims and practice procedure will help develop the practical application of many of the ideas and concepts presented in Lesson Eighteen. This procedure should be applied to the practice of pieces and exercises. Practice should be slow and careful to allow control to develop.

Chromatic octaves in the first position (Exercise 81) offer an excellent opportunity to explore the implications of this practice technique.

Aims

1) **Smoothness:** Develop an even and fluid motion of the fingers, hand, forearm, and elbow. The cultivation of smooth left-hand movements will aid the development of the right hand. Avoid awkward and jerky movements.

2) **Preparation/Anticipation:** Develop the control of the left-hand fingers so they can prepare for their next notes wherever possible. When not possible, left-hand fingers should begin to move toward their notes to anticipate them.

3) **Maximum Mechanical Advantage:** Arrive at a position of the greatest mechanical advantage through a consideration of the alignment and midrange principles.

4) **Accuracy:** Train the fingers to stop notes directly behind the fret. Remember that accuracy will depend on the hand being in a position of greatest mechanical advantage.

Procedure

1) Position the fingers on the first octave. Make sure the wrist is aligned with the forearm and the finger joints are as close as possible to their midrange position. Listen carefully to the quality and clarity of the sound.

2) Think ahead to the next octave. Imagine what new positions, if any, need to be assumed by the fingers, wrist, forearm, and elbow in playing the new notes. Is there an opportunity for fingers to prepare notes beforehand? Are any fingers free to anticipate notes? Can the hand pivot on a fixed finger into its new position? The ease of playing chromatic octaves can be enhanced by understanding the importance of the hand's ability to pivot on a fixed finger. Every time an octave contains an open string, positioning

can be improved for the next octave by moving the elbow toward the body if the fourth finger is to be positioned on the lower string, and away from the body if the fourth finger is to be positioned on the higher string. These movements, combined with rotation of the forearm, can be performed while the notes of the first octave are still sounding.

3) Move slowly and smoothly to the new notes. As the fingers and hand move to the next notes, they should begin to assume whatever new position (if any) may be needed to play accurately.

4) Left-hand movements should be timed to allow the left hand and fingers to reach their optimum position as the fingers are placed behind their frets.

Exercise 81:

The next sixteen exercises gradually increase the reach across the strings. As the size of the intervals increases, the movements of the left forearm and elbow will need to be more pronounced to bring the fingertips to their strings—avoid excessive reaching with the fingers. Less experienced students may want to begin these exercises in a higher position where the distance between the frets is less. Start with the easiest form of each exercise: stay in one position or with the version that reaches across fewer strings until thoroughly mastered.

Notes on adjacent strings may be played with *i* and *m* together. Exercises involving wider intervals provide an excellent opportunity to practice an *m-a* alternation on the upper strings while *p* plays the lower strings.

Exercise 82:

II

III

Continue through seventh position.

Exercise 83:

I

II

III

Continue through seventh position.

Exercise 84:

Continue through
seventh position.

Exercise 85:

Continue through
seventh position.

Exercise 86:

Continue through
seventh position.

Exercise 87:

Continue through
seventh position.

Exercise 88:

II

III

Continue through seventh position.

Exercise 89:

II

III

Continue through seventh position.

86

Exercise 90:

Continue through seventh position.

Exercise 91:

Continue through seventh position.

Exercise 92:

Continue through seventh position.

87

Exercise 93:

Continue through
seventh position.

Exercise 94:

Continue through
seventh position.

Exercise 95:

Continue through
seventh position.

Exercise 96:

Continue through
seventh position.

Exercise 97:

Continue through
seventh position.

The following six exercises help develop finger independence while other fingers are fixed. As in the previous exercises, use the movements of the left arm to help position the fingers.

Exercise 98:

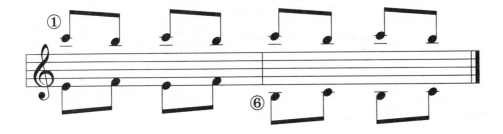

Repeat each measure 2-4
times. Descend to first
position.

Exercise 99:

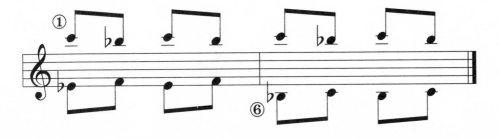

Repeat each measure 2-4
times. Descend to first
position.

Exercise 100:

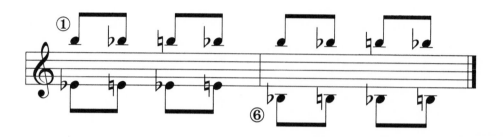

Repeat each measure 2-4 times. Descend to first position.

Exercise 101:

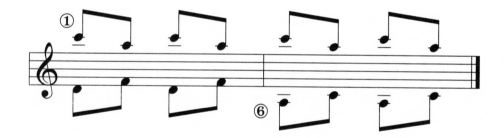

Repeat each measure 2-4 times. Descend to first position.

Exercise 102:

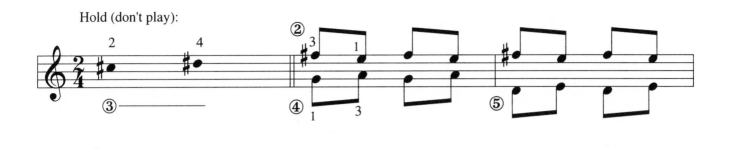

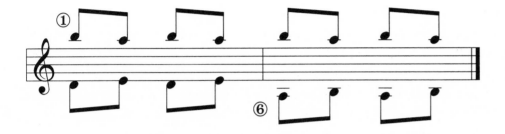

Repeat each measure 2-4 times. Descend to first position.

Exercise 103:

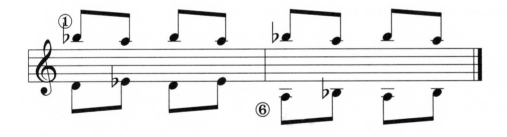

Repeat each measure 2-4 times. Descend to first position.

Lesson Twenty

Slurs

Left-hand slurs are not really difficult once effective left-hand positions and finger movements have been cultivated. Problems usually arise when the left-hand fingers are not placed in an advantageous position and are thus unable to move comfortably and accurately. Problems of positioning and movement, more than any inherent difficulties with slurs themselves, contribute to the mistaken belief that slur technique calls for an excessive amount of left hand force. The material about the positioning and movement of the left hand and fingers should be a part of technique before the study of slurs can begin.

When performing an ascending slur, the finger joints should be positioned in their midrange position and the finger should move onto the string primarily from the knuckle joint. The hand should be positioned so that the fingertip can fall directly behind the fret. Avoid reaching with the finger.

The movement for a descending slur is *not* the opposite of the movement for an ascending slur. When performing a descending slur, the fingertip should be positioned directly behind the fret, and a simultaneous flexion of the middle and tip joints should occur. It is this movement that will cause the string to sound. Some extension from the knuckle joint will be needed to allow the finger to clear the upper adjacent string.[114]

Practice Information

The following exercises use simple left-hand finger patterns. More advanced formulae may be devised later. The repetition of these patterns on each string will help build endurance and will allow you to concentrate on the position and movement of the fingers. Ascend to the ninth position. To build velocity or to practice left-hand string crossing, more advanced students should practice the variations given after each exercise.

---

114) See Shearer, 98, for some useful information on descending slurs.

Ascending Slurs

Exercise 104:

Continue.

Exercise 105:

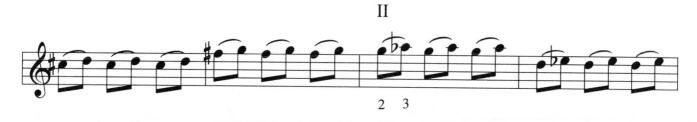

Continue.

A.

B.

94

Exercise 106:

Continue.

A.

95

Exercise 107:

II

Continue.

A.

II

B.

Exercise 108:

Continue.

Exercise 109:

Continue.

A.

Exercise 110:

Continue.

Exercise 111:

Continue.

Exercise 112:

Continue.

Exercise 113:

Continue.

Exercise 114:

Continue.

Descending Slurs

Exercise 115:

II

Continue.

A.

B.

Exercise 116:

II

Continue.

A.

II

B.

101

Exercise 117:

II

Continue.

A.

II

B.

Exercise 118:

II

Continue.

A.

103

Exercise 119:

II

Continue.

A.

B.

II

Exercise 120:

II

Continue.

A.

II

B.

105

Exercise 121:

Continue.

Exercise 122:

Continue.

Exercise 123:

Continue.

Exercise 124:

Continue.

Exercise 125:

Continue.

Slurs Across Two Strings

Guitar music occasionally contains ascending and descending slurs across two strings. When descending, the right hand plays the first note and the left-hand finger strikes the lower note with enough force to cause it to sound. These are called "vibration" or "echo" slurs by Matteo Carcassi and Ferdinando Carulli respectively. Ascending slurs across two strings are performed by gently gliding the right-hand thumb from the first note to the second. Although their legato articulation does suggest a slur, these ascending "slurs" are not really slurs. The following examples from Carcassi's *Guitar Method* illustrate these techniques.

Slurs across two strings were used with frequency in the Nineteenth-Century literature for solo guitar.

Slurs Across Two Strings:

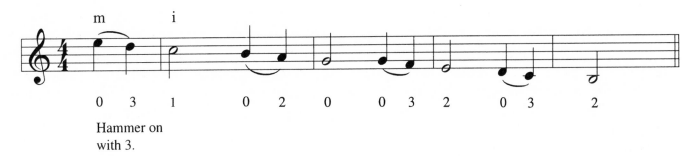

Hammer on
with 3.

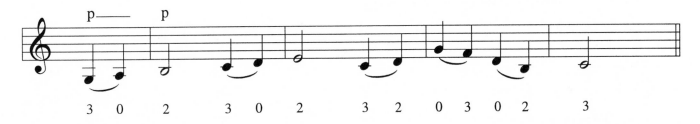

Glide upwards
with p.

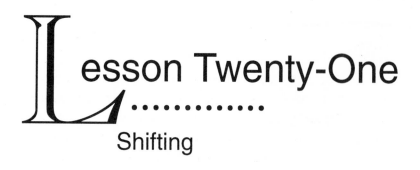

Lesson Twenty-One

Shifting

Effortless and transparent shifts should be the goal of all guitarists wishing to develop a musically sensitive technique. Yet too often, poorly performed shifts add unwanted accents and contribute to choppy and disjointed phrasing. The use of a "free finger" shift will let you shift into a new position with a finger that is not under tension.[115]

In the first part of the following example, substitute the second finger for the third and then gently slide into the new position. In the second part of the example, practice the finger substitution and the shift simultaneously. The shifts should be anticipated by the movement of the elbow—the hand will then follow. The movement of the elbow comes from the shoulder—the shoulder itself should not move. Do not hold the note until the last possible instant and then move rapidly to the new position—avoid sudden or jerky movements. Tension created by the opposing muscular force needed to stop these movements is often transferred to the right-hand fingers as an involuntary accent.

The technique of anticipating a shift with movement from the arm and then letting the fingers follow can be applied to all musical textures, not just scales.

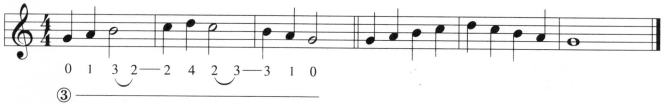

The same concepts can be applied to other shifts as well:

Playing major scales on a single string is an excellent way to study these shifts.

Exercise 126:

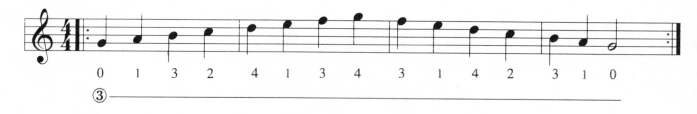

---

115) See Aaron Shearer's *Scale Pattern Studies for Guitar*, (Melville, NY: Belwin-Mills, 1965), 252. This may be the first systematic explanation and use of this type of shift.

The following scale exercises on two strings cover numerous shifting possibilities. Begin slowly and try to make each shift inaudible. Let the arm anticipate each shift with a slight movement of the elbow and let the hand follow. Gradually increase the speed. For added variety, use the rhythmic variants presented in Lesson Twenty-Three. Ascend to the eleventh position for the major, lydian, and mixolydian modes and to the twelfth position for the others.

Exercise 127: Major

Exercise 128: Harmonic Minor

Exercise 129: Melodic Minor

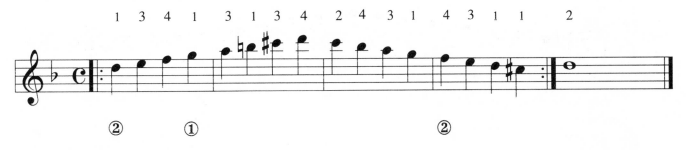

Exercise 130: Dorian Mode

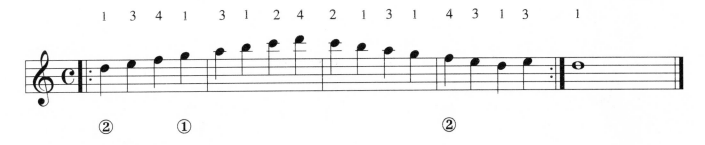

Exercise 131: Phrygian Mode

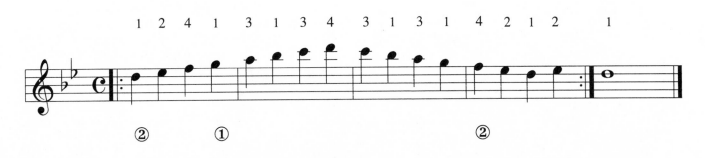

109

Exercise 132: Lydian Mode

Exercise 133: Mixolydian Mode

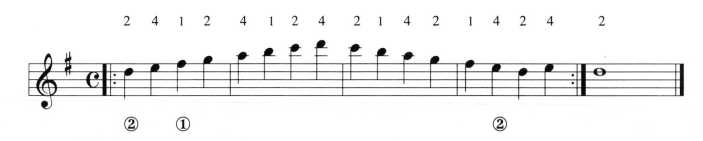

Exercise 134: Aeolian Mode (Natural Minor)

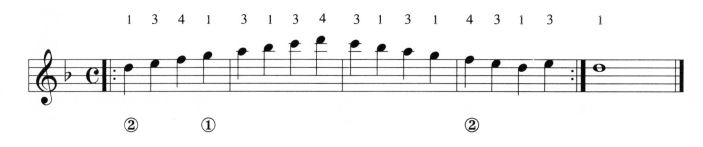

Lesson Twenty-Two

Long Scales

Andrés Segovia wrote in the preface to his *Diatonic Major and Minor Scales:* "The practice of scales enables one to solve a greater number of technical problems in a shorter time than the study of any other exercise."[116] Long scales, that is, scales that traverse the *length* of the fingerboard, are particularly well suited for technical study: they pose problems of timing and coordination between the hands, string crossing, shifting, and later, speed and endurance.

Long scales fall into two groups: two octave scales starting on the fifth string and three octave scales starting on the sixth string. Wherever possible, free finger shifts are used on the treble strings. Fingerings are the same for all two octave scales of the same kind and are presented the first time a form occurs in the circle of fifths. There are several exceptions for the three octave scales. Where needed, these fingerings are given.

Scales should be practiced rest stroke and free stroke with the following right-hand finger combinations: *i-m, m-i, m-a, a-m, i-a,* and *a-i*. More advanced students can also study these scales with *a-m-i* and *i-m-a-m*.

The scales should be practiced staccato at first. This is simply the prepared stroke applied to scale playing: the staccato is caused by the preparation of *both* the right and the left-hand fingers. The left-hand finger preparation is needed to create a uniform staccato when crossing strings. The length of the staccato can vary from slightly less than a quarter note to a thirty-second note. This will allow the speed of finger movements to increase without increasing the tempo.

C Major: staccato

More advanced practice routines are presented in Lesson Twenty-Three.

---

116) Andrés Segovia, *Diatonic Major and Minor Scales* (Washington D.C.: Columbia Music Co., 1953), 1.

Major Scales

C Major:

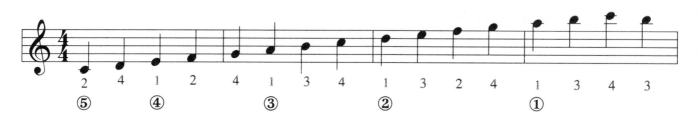

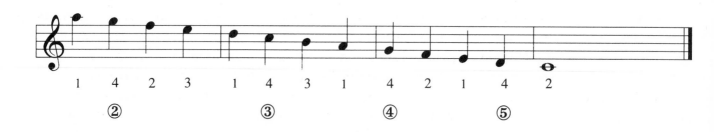

G Major:

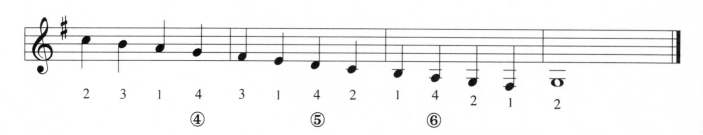

D Major:

A Major:

E Major:

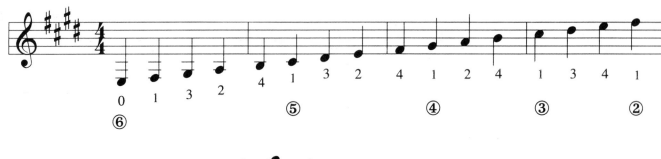

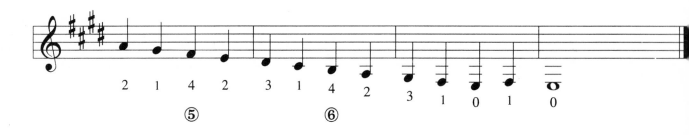

B Major:

F Sharp Major:

D Flat Major:

A Flat Major:

E Flat Major:

116

B Flat Major:

F Major:

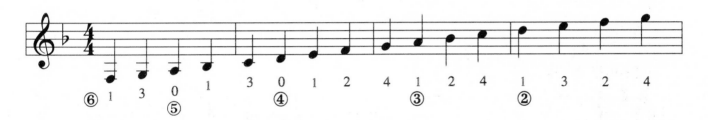

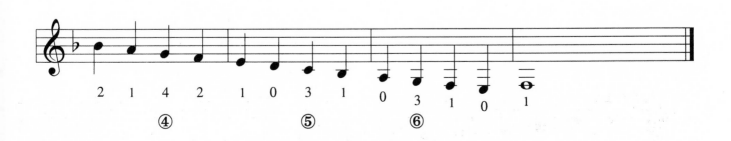

117

Melodic Minor Scales

A Melodic Minor:

E Melodic Minor:

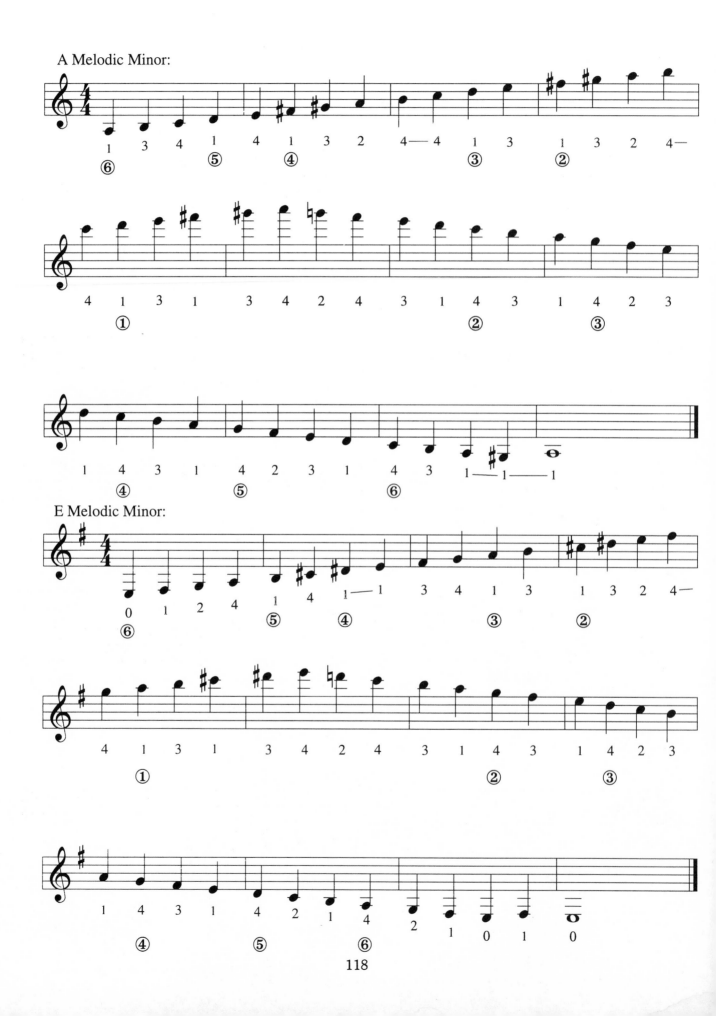

B Melodic Minor:

F Sharp Melodic Minor:

119

C Sharp Melodic Minor:

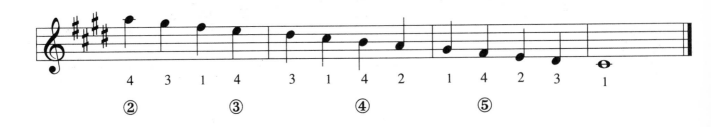

G Sharp Melodic Minor:

D Sharp Melodic Minor:

B Flat Melodic Minor:

F Melodic Minor:

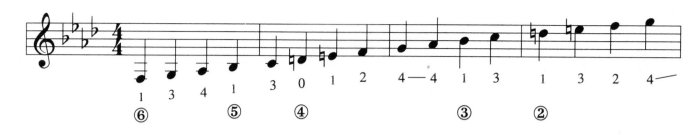

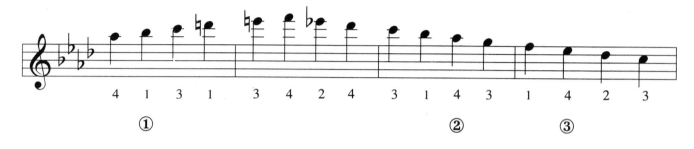

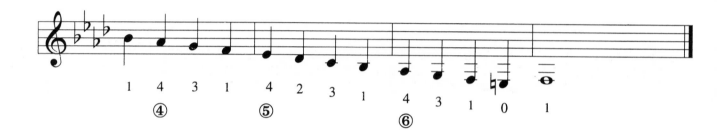

C Melodic Minor:

122

G Melodic Minor:

D Melodic Minor:

Harmonic Minor Scales

A Harmonic Minor:

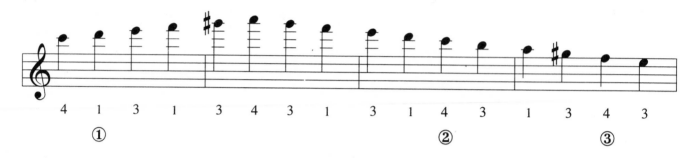

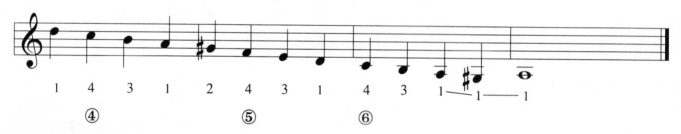

E Harmonic Minor:

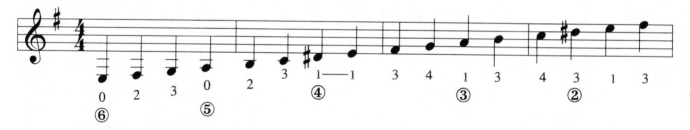

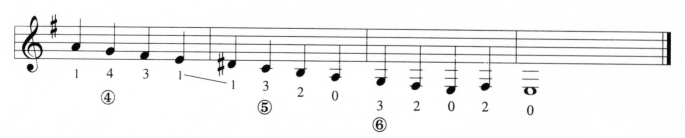

B Harmonic Minor:

F Sharp Harmonic Minor:

C Sharp Harmonic Minor:

G Sharp Harmonic Minor:

D Sharp Harmonic Minor:

B Flat Harmonic Minor:

F Harmonic Minor:

127

C Harmonic Minor:

G Harmonic Minor:

D Harmonic Minor:

Lesson Twenty-Three

Scale Practice

One Octave Scale Exercises

These short daily scale exercises can be played only once or repeated and practiced many times in a session. These exercises use one octave major and minor scales as well as modes. This will accustom the left hand to a wider variety of finger patterns.

Practice the exercises slowly at first. Study the release of each finger and keep the strokes free of tension. This will be essential if high speeds are to be attained. Make sure your string crossing is working well. The rhythmic variants given for the major scale should also be applied to the minor scales and modes. These will help lead to fluency and later serve as models for the practice of two and three octave long scales.

Advanced students can eliminate the rhythmic variants but should be sure to practice each scale in triplets and sextuplets as well as groups of four sixteenth notes.

A wide variety of right-hand fingerings can be used (see Lesson Fourteen for an explanation of the movements for the three-finger patterns).

m-i	a-m-i (start with m for major,
i-m	lydian, and mixolydian.)
a-m	i-m-a
m-a	i-m-a-m
a-i	a-i-m-i
i-a	i-a-m-a

The "sliding apoyando" should be practiced rest stroke only. The finger will slide from one string to the next when playing two consecutive descending notes on adjacent strings. The finger will need to make an adjustment to find its contact point for the second note. Eventually the two notes are executed in one continuous and fluid movement.[117]

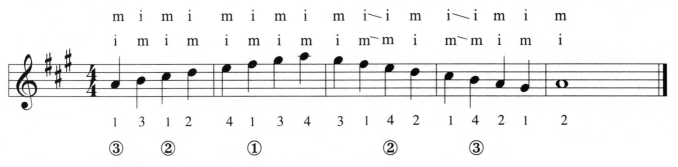

Scales with the thumb and index finger should be practiced free stroke only.

---

117) Also see Romero, 34.

Do not think that you should be able to practice all possibilities in a practice session. Be flexible. Occasionally practice some of the more complex right-hand fingerings but keep track of your best and most secure fingerings and use those when you are working on speed. If you find a pattern you want to work on more, repeat it in successively higher positions. These exercises will help your technique become more well-rounded.

These exercises can also serve as models for practicing difficult sections of pieces.

Exercise 135: Major

Exercise 135a:

Exercise 135b:

Exercise 135c:

Exercise 135d:

Exercise 135e:

Exercise 135f:

Exercise 135g:

Exercise 135h:

Exercise 135i:

Exercise 135j:

Exercise 135k:

Exercise 135l:

Exercise 135m:

Exercise 135n:

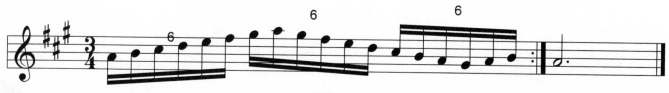

Exercise 136: Harmonic Minor

Exercise 137: Melodic Minor

Exercise 138: Dorian Mode

Exercise 139: Phrygian Mode

Exercise 140: Lydian Mode

Exercise 141: Mixolydian Mode

Exercise 142: Aeolian Mode (Natural Minor)

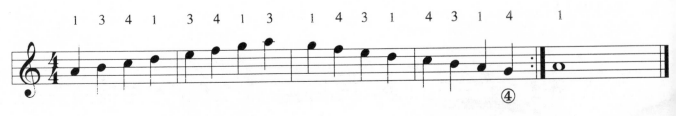

Two and Three Octave Scale Exercises

The following practice routines can be beneficial for developing advanced technique. Start at a slow tempo and increase the metronome speed for each change of position or each time through the complete exercise. These exercises should be studied with rest stroke and free stroke. Although most students will find *i-m* or *m-i* the most comfortable right-hand fingering, other combinations should not be neglected.

Experiment with the rhythmic variants presented above.

Exercise 143: Major

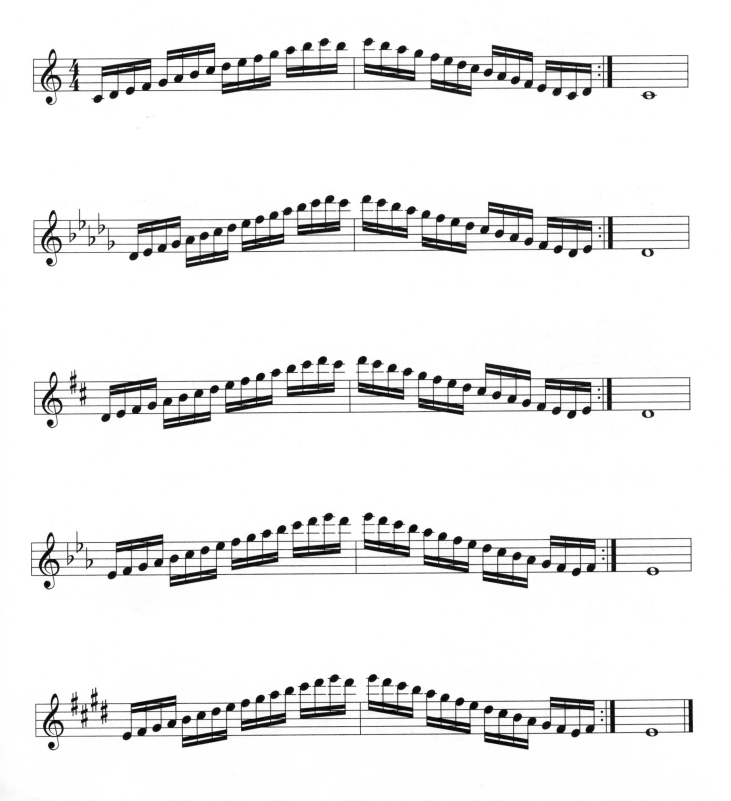

Exercise 144: Melodic Minor

Continue and ascend through the seventh position.

Exercise 145: Harmonic Minor

Continue and ascend through the seventh position.

Exercise 146: Major

Continue and ascend through the sixth position.

Exercise 147: Melodic Minor

Continue and ascend through the seventh position.

Exercise 148: Harmonic Minor

Continue and ascend through the seventh position.

Lesson Twenty-four

Scale Exercises for Speed and Effortless Endurance

These exercises can teach you to maintain your speed over increasingly longer periods of time. The first exercise in each group requires short "bursts" of speed. Take advantage of the opportunity to relax the fingers during the longer notes. The next exercise extends that burst slightly and the final exercise requires the comfortable endurance to maintain the speed throughout.

Exercises in major keys should ascend through the sixth position and exercises in harmonic minor keys should ascend through the seventh position. The melodic minor scales are not well suited for this type of study.

Remain in position while repeating measures. This may require a change of fingering.

Exercises of Two Octaves

Exercise 149a: Major

Repeat four times.

Repeat four times.

136

Exercise 149b:

Repeat four times.

Repeat four times.

Exercise 149c:

Repeat four times.

Repeat four times.

Exercise 150a: Harmonic Minor

Repeat four times.

Repeat four times.

Exercise 150b:

Repeat four times.

Repeat four times.

Exercise 150c:

Repeat four times.

Repeat four times.

Exercises of Three Octaves

Exercise 151a: Major

Repeat four times.

Repeat four times.

Exercise 151b:

Repeat four times.

Repeat four times.

Exercise 151c:

Repeat four times.

Repeat four times.

Exercise 152a: Harmonic Minor

Repeat four times.

Repeat four times.

Exercise 152b:

Repeat four times.

Repeat four times.

Exercise 152c:

Repeat four times.

Repeat four times.

Appendices

Appendix One: Tuning[118]

The guitar is made to be tuned in equal temperament, a system of tuning that divides the octave into twelve equal semitones. No interval besides the octave (or unison) is acoustically correct. Further, although many guitarists prefer to tune using harmonics (the sounds are of similar colors and the beats between pitches are clearer), the only natural harmonics that are "in tune" with equal temperament are octave harmonics which are produced at the fifth and twelfth frets.

The method of tuning that uses natural harmonics produced at the seventh fret will yield unsatisfactory results: these harmonics are an *acoustically perfect* fifth above the open string. The *well-tempered* fifth is 2 cents larger, (equal temperament divides each semitone into 100 cents). Although this difference is too small to hear, the error becomes compounded as tuning proceeds across the strings. The difference is much more significant with intervals of a third: the well-tempered third is 14 cents larger than the pure third.

The harmonics used in the following tuning procedure will help you tune with precision. The combination of natural and artificial harmonics will allow the guitar to be tuned in equal temperament. After tuning the fifth string to a tuning fork, tune the second note of each measure to the first.

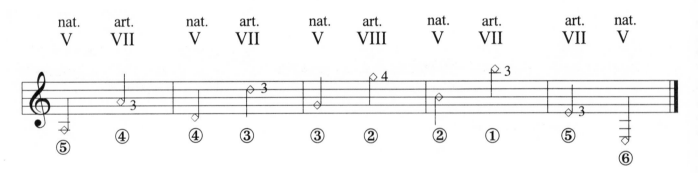

In his *Guitar Method,* Matteo Carcassi recommended checking the tuning with the following octaves:

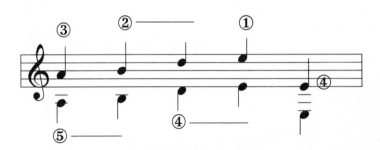

118) For a more detailed explanation of guitar tuning see David Dolata, "The Secret of Tuning by Harmonics," *The Soundboard, Journal of the Guitar Foundation of America,* Vol. 19, No.4, Spring, 1993, 27-37.

Appendix Two: For Further Study

General Study

There is a scarcity of books dealing with the fundamental mechanics of guitar study. One book of interest is *The Natural Classical Guitar,* by Lee F. Ryan (Westport, CT: The Bold Strummer, LTD, 1991). The discussions of mind-body awareness, concentration, and visualization are quite useful. I am less enthusiastic about his discussions of the mechanical aspects of technique.

Pepe Romero offers some valuable observations, particularly about right-hand technique, in his *Guitar Style and Technique* (New York: Bradley Publications, 1982).

Hector Quine's *Guitar Technique* (New York: Oxford University Press, 1990) has some useful information. Although Quine invokes "physiological fact" to support his principles and ideas, some of his physiological information is either missing or inaccurate.

John Duarte's *Foundation Studies in Classic Guitar Technique* (Borough Green, Sevenoaks, Kent: Novello and Company Ltd., 1966) is not a technical text but offers a wealth of exercises and practice information for the study of scales, slurs, arpeggios, and chord forms.

The best method for beginners is unquestionably Aaron Shearer's *Learning the Classic Guitar,* Parts One and Two (Pacific, MO: Mel Bay Publications, Inc., 1990). Shearer's presentation of material is excellent. Part One is a technical text and even advanced students are encouraged to study Shearer's approach. Part Two contains music and many of the pieces can be used as supplemental material to the lessons presented in this book. Shearer's "Table of Contents" is very clear and students should have little trouble locating the pieces they need. Part Three (Pacific, MO: Mel Bay Publications, Inc., 1991) is an excellent introduction to music interpretation.

Two books that present excellent introductions to the Alexander Technique are *Body Learning,* by Michael Gelb (New York: Henry Holt and Company, 1987) and *The Alexander Technique,* by Judith Leibowitz and Bill Connington (New York: Harper and Row, 1990). Although the Alexander Technique cannot be learned from a book, these books contain good information about tension and habits of positioning and movement.

Tone Deaf and All Thumbs? by Frank R. Wilson (New York, NY: Vintage Books, 1987) is a fascinating exploration of music making undertaken by a neurologist. Of special interest are Chapters Two and Three.

As I was putting the finishing touches on this book, I came across *You Are Your Instrument: The Definitive Musician's Guide to Practice and Performance* by Julie Lyonn Liebermann (New York, NY: Huisiki Music, 1991). This is a wonderfully holistic approach to the musician's problems. I loved it.

Lesson One: Seating

Guitarists are encouraged to explore seating and positioning the guitar without a footstool. The most convenient device is the **Guitar A-Frame Support** available from Mel Bay Publications (Call 1-800-8-MEL BAY for a Complete Catalog). This product is light, inexpensive, and offers a wide range of positioning options.

Lesson Fifteen: Giuliani Revisited

Giuliani, Mauro, *Studio per la chitarra, opus 1. The Complete Works, Vol. 1,* ed. Brian Jeffery (London: Tecla Editions, 1984). This is a facsimile of the original 1812 edition.

Berg, Christopher, *Guiliani Revisited* (Pacific, MO: Mel Bay Publications, Inc., 1997). This book is an update of Giuliani's work. Many new patterns have been included based on pieces composed since Giuliani's time.

Serious guitarists should also study the numerous arpeggio studies of Carcassi, Carulli, Giuliani, and Sor. They are widely available in various editions.

Lesson Nineteen: Independence Exercises

Carlevaro, Abel, *Serie Didactica para Guitarra,* Cuaderno No. 4. (Buenos Aires: Barry, 1974). The latter part of this book offers some good supplementary left-hand exercises.

Shearer, Aaron, *Slur, Ornament and Reach Development Exercises* (Melville, NY: Belwin-Mills, 1969). The last section, "Reach Control Development Exercises for the Left Hand," presents many excellent exercises for further study.

Lesson Twenty: Slurs

Carlevaro, Abel, *Serie Didactica para Guitarra,* Cuaderno No. 4. (Buenos Aires: Barry, 1974). The first part of this work offers many slur exercises.

Segovia, Andrés, *Slur Exercises and Chromatic Octaves* (Washington, DC: Columbia Music Co., 1970). This standard work is an excellent source of more advanced slur exercises.

Shearer, Aaron, *Slur, Ornament and Reach Development Exercises* (Melville, NY: Belwin-Mills, 1969). This book offers many valuable exercises for beginning and advanced students.

Lesson Twenty-Two: Long Scales

Segovia, Andrés, *Diatonic Major and Minor Scales* (Washington, DC: Columbia Music Co., 1953). What are popularly termed the "Segovia scales" are widely studied by guitar students. But Segovia revealed in his autobiography he worked out the fingerings to these scales some time prior to his 1909 debut at age sixteen. While his fingerings are an excellent source of difficult shifts, they may not be the best fingerings for developing a smooth and fluid scale technique. Students who already practice the Segovia scales and do not wish to change fingerings can, of course, still practice the routines presented in Lessons Twenty-Three and Twenty-Four.

It should be clear that although long scales are excellent for the practice of technique, their value as a means to mastery of the fingerboard is limited. For a thorough study of major and minor scales in *all* the positions, students are referred to Aaron Shearer's *Scale Pattern Studies for Guitar* (Melville, NY: Belwin-Mills, 1965). The bulk of this work is devoted to the study of the five major, melodic minor, and harmonic minor scale forms in each position.